B12   1250

SYLVIA MANN

Collecting Playing Cards

BELL PUBLISHING COMPANY · NEW YORK

To the memory of
WILLIAM PENN
a most excellent collector and friend

This edition published by Bell Publishing Company, Inc.,
a division of Crown Publishers, Inc.
A   B   C   D   E   F   G   H

CONTENTS

PLATES

7

INTRODUCTION

THE EARLY history of playing cards is fraught with speculation and offers endless possibilities for unrewarding controversy. Fortunately for the collector, such history (prior to A.D. 1500, that is) can be relegated to the realms of academic fantasy, for he or she is unlikely ever to find cards from an earlier time outside a museum.

A précis of the scraps of information which relate to the earliest cards would yield little more than the fact that they were established in Italy, France and Germany by the late fourteenth century, that they were hand-made, often beautifully illuminated and were the prerogative of royalty or the wealthy aristocracy. In the fifteenth century, with the advent of woodblock printing and the accompanying development of a pioneer system of mass-production, cards became less beautiful, less expensive and universally popular. By the end of that century they had been denounced as a work of the devil by practically everyone in authority—including saints, kings, mayors and landowners who required people to work when in fact all they wanted was a game of cards.

By the sixteenth century, however, cards had become respectable and were generally accepted as part of the social scene. In England, for example, the Pastons were playing with them, Henry VII's queen was losing money at them (much to her parsimonious husband's annoyance), and cardmakers were protected by law from a flood of imported cards from abroad. Millions of packs of cards were being produced by thousands of makers all over Europe and it is at this stage in the history of playing cards that the collector can begin to take a personal interest. Only begin, perhaps, because sixteenth-century cards are still an almost once-in-a-lifetime discovery, but by this time the form that cards were to take was more or less established, and many of the different packs used throughout Europe at the

9

present time have designs which are directly descended from patterns used three or four hundred years ago. Today the geography of Europe in many bygone periods is reflected by the cards used in different parts of the world. Cards found in Macao, for instance, sometimes resemble those known also in Brazil: both packs owe their form to an original in Portugal when it was a great colonial power. Nearer home, standard English cards have features known also in very old cards from Guienne, Brittany and the Low Countries: our king of hearts, for example, is the king of money in a provincial pack in northern Italy.

There is more, however, to the collecting of playing cards than confirmation of known geographical-cum-historical maps —although I personally find this a quite fascinating aspect of the hobby. For as well as the standard types of card used by the general public for mere gaming, from a very early period many other types of pack were produced for a variety of purposes— artistic, political, educational, comical, some even verging on appealing to a penchant for scurrility. These types of card provide a contemporary view of many ages unsurpassed in popular or indeed other art. The violence and virulence of religious intolerance in England in the seventeenth century is portrayed unforgettably on a slanderous pack of fifty-two cards illustrating the pretended Popish Plot. A critical eye is cast on the South Sea and other Bubbles in four different packs made in England and Holland in the following century. A snobbish preoccupation with heraldry resulted in many packs of cards depicting coats-of-arms (this fashion was followed in Scotland, England, Germany, France, Italy and Spain). Geographical packs can provide fifty-two contemporary eighteenth-century maps and commentaries (and very quaint some of their ideas of the world seem to have been).

Like every lasting commodity, there are fashions in cards, and these fashions very often reflect the history of the times— during the French revolution, court cards had their crowns and sceptre-heads removed; the poverty of French army authorities in the Anglo-French war in Canada compelled them to issue 'card money' as pay. Tarot cards, which originated in medieval Italy (whatever you may hear to the contrary), depict a great deal of Christian religious symbolism and many preoccupations of the age. Certain types of card issued in the Austro-Hungarian Empire reflected the craze for *chinoiserie* which prevailed throughout Europe in the early part of the nineteenth century: and in our own times cards are sometimes produced as part of an advertising campaign for, say, Roger et Gallet, Hoover, Neiman-Marcus of Dallas, *Time Magazine*, J. Lyons, etc.

Perhaps it would be wise, at this point, having established the existence of such a wide variety in the world of card playing, to come to some sort of understanding as to what a collector can collect and what the term 'playing card' involves. My own search is a general one, for cards which have a number of different suits, each containing cards with a series of ascending values, unlike card games which do not (Happy Families, Animal Grab, etc.), of any period or country, provided that each pack is different from those already in my collection. Some people collect the designs on the backs of cards, either indiscriminately or thematically, some people collect jokers only, some collect cards of one country only, some collect *fronts* of cards thematically—one famous collection has been made of cards having war as their subject. This book, however, is not intended so much for the specialist as for the general collector who might benefit from my experiences and may, I hope, share some of the pleasure which collecting cards has given me for a number of years: also, perhaps, it may spark off some enthusiasm for specialization or research.

The first thing with which the collector should familiarize himself is the formation and distribution of the various European suit-systems. In England, insular and conservative as we are, we have only one style of card—one which, incidentally, bears French suit-marks with anglicized names. There are, however, on the continent a number of other suit-systems which are as old, if not older than our own.

It is thought likely that suits basically represent different factions or estates in medieval life—for example, the church,

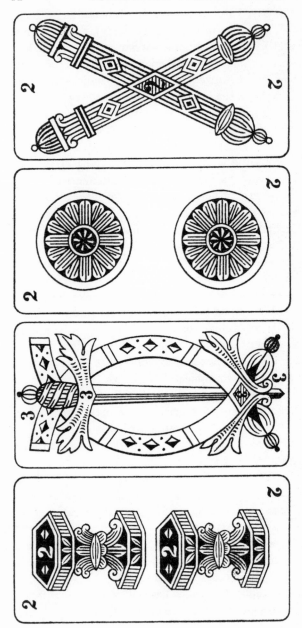

Fig. 1. Conventional Italian suit-marks; *coppe* (cups), *spade* (swords), *denari* (money) and *bastoni* (batons or clubs).

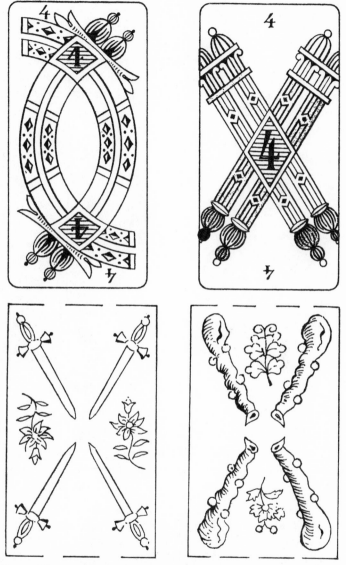

Fig. 2. The top two cards show the Italian arrangement of sword and club pips on cards. The lower two show the Spanish arrangement: note also the line breaks in the border.

the army, the merchants and the peasantry. Whether or not this is so, it might well explain the etymological and other links that the systems have with each other.

In Italy at least this theory seems to hold good. Purely Italian suits, which are used only in north-east Italy and any part of the world to which the two Italian games of *tarocco* and *trappola* have spread, are shown in fig. 1.

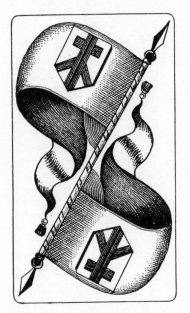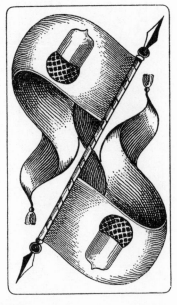

Fig. 3A. Swiss suit-marks are *Wappenschilden* (shields), *Eicheln* (acorns), *Schellen* (hawkbells) and Blumen (flowers).

The first point to notice here is the Italian word for a sword—a word which in anglicized form rather confusingly refers to the French emblem of the military suit. The original French suits are those found on English cards today, known in France as *coeurs* (hearts), *piques* (pikes), *carreaux* (paving tiles) and *trèfles* (trefoils)—our hearts, spades, diamonds and clubs respectively.

The English adopted the French suit-marks but, apart from

the heart suit, in naming them adopted the spirit of the Italian
suits: spades from the Italian word, diamonds from the idea of
riches, and clubs from the batons. England is about the only
country to mingle the two systems to this extent: the rest of
Europe follows France's lead, although the Dutch and Scandi-
navians refer to paving-tiles as window-panes and follow
England's lead over the military suit (Denmark and Sweden

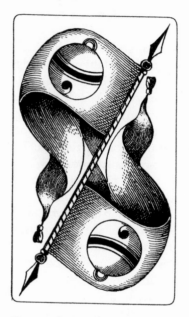

Fig. 3B. Swiss suit-marks are shown here on the banner card of each
suit, the ancient equivalent of a 10.

spader, Norway *spar*), and the Italians call the trefoil suit
'flowers'.

The Spanish suit-system is very closely linked to the Italian
and in fact in parts of Italy where Spanish rule existed, the
Spanish markings persist. The names are more or less the same,
although the presentation of the swords and clubs is distinctive.

The Spanish swords and clubs are not merely shaped differently from the Italian, they are also arranged on the cards quite differently. Italian symbols for these suits intertwine, whereas Spanish symbols are delineated separately: see fig. 2.

The two remaining suit systems are also closely linked one with the other, namely the Swiss and the German. These, however, are linked only very tenuously with other European systems. Swiss suit-marks are shown in figs. 3A and 3B.

German suit-marks are similar, but substitute hearts for shields and leaves for flowers.

Although to many people suit-systems other than the French seem strange, they are still in use today (although bridge, canasta and poker cards—which follow the English pattern— must inevitably be in the majority everywhere). However, local games require local cards and almost any traveller in Europe today, if he or she visits a non-tourist café, will find the local people playing with cards which are traditional in the area. This does not simply mean different suit-marks from our own but also different arrangements and patterns of those suit-marks peculiar to a country or district. Part of the charm of card-collecting lies in the fact that in so many parts of the world cards can be bought, the patterns of which have been in use in the locality for centuries. Even if you cannot trace an old version of a pack—and many are elusive—you may very well be able to obtain its modern counterpart as representative of the species. Exactly where one can expect to find each pattern of card will be examined in later chapters dealing with individual countries. Generally speaking, however, Italian and Italo-Spanish cards can be found in the Italian peninsula, Yugoslavia, Switzerland and S.E. France; Spanish suits in Spain, Catalan France and Brittany; Swiss national suits in parts of Switzerland; German suits in southern and eastern Germany, Poland and the area covered by the old Austro-Hungarian Empire. In these countries as well as practically all others, cards with French suits can also be found.

This leads us to the ever-pressing problem; how does one collect playing cards? First, it must be said that cards very rarely appear on the open market. Those that do tend nowadays to be expensive although prices are not comparable with more widely collected items such as stamps or coins. A pack of sixteenth century Italian cards fetched £220 at Sotheby's in 1963 and several rare seventeenth and eighteenth century packs get priced at between £50 and £200, but these figures are quite exceptional. The *collector* of playing cards must use his own ingenuity and initiative to seek out items from a wide variety of sources. For instance, although most people may not have observed this, at the time of writing it is possible to buy in Great Britain, new, over the counter, at least a dozen different packs of cards with varying degrees of artistic merit, none of which remotely resembles our familiar standard design. Standard cards are also available which have been imported from the U.S.A., Belgium, Germany, Czechoslovakia, China and Austria. It is always worthwhile for a collector to glance at any cards on sale. A year or so ago I found some packs of patience cards made in Czechoslovakia, with a most unusual and charming design, in a small stationer's in a provincial town. I have since heard that this design is known in its native country, but I have never found any other collector who has traced the exported version.

Next, one should not forget the junk shops. These are becoming less rewarding as they become grander and specialize in furniture and household wares, and the day of the genuine junk shop is nearly over. But they are still worth a visit. Antique dealers only very occasionally have packs of cards—but here again, never ignore them: sometimes old packs turn up in odd pieces of furniture and go at a reasonable price. The same argument applies to second-hand book or print shops: a pack may be included in a mixed lot, and a dealer will probably sell it at a reasonable price.

Another useful source of supply is friends. It is astonishing how many people at one stage or another have had a pack of unusual cards introduced into their house. German patience cards bought on holiday, old Spanish cards handed down in the family, Russian cards owned by great-uncles in St Petersburg,

Diamond Jubilee cards kept along with other Victoriana, five-suit bridge cards received as unwanted Christmas presents before 1939. Friends travelling abroad will often buy cards from a local tobacconist (in most European countries). It is advisable to write down the name of the pack you would like in the appropriate language. If you travel abroad yourself, look in print shops and booksellers, as well as tobacconists (stationers in Switzerland). Bargains do occasionally turn up: I myself have found a pack of seventeenth-century heraldic cards bound in book form, with only one card missing, which cost me thirty-five shillings.

The surest source of supply, however, is by trading with other collectors, usually in other countries. These collectors can be contacted by joining either or both of the playing card collectors' organizations which exist in the U.S.A.;[1] the small subscription can be paid through any bank and all members receive a roster of names and addresses of other members and also a note of the types of cards they collect. I have acquired many packs quite new to me in this way, and have even received nearly forty packs from behind the Iron Curtain. The beginner may feel short of trading material at first, but a small expenditure on the non-standard packs available in this country will quickly prove a good investment. The De La Rue tercentenary issue of 1960, commemorating the accession of Charles II, brought me several unusual items from Czechoslovakia, Belgium and the U.S.A. The clubs also hold postal auctions from time to time, and a modest bid sometimes brings in a nice antique item (a bank can arrange for payment of purchases from abroad).

Another method of obtaining cards is by advertising for them, but I have found this rather costly, and the expenditure is quite out of proportion to the goods received.

Once the initial steps have been taken and the nucleus of a

[1] The Playing Card Collectors' Assoc. Inc., with headquarters in Milwaukee, Wisconsin, and The Chicago Playing Card Collectors Inc., 9645 S. Leavitt Street, Chicago 43.

collection has been formed, there come the immediate problems of display, storage and indexing.

My own view regarding display is that the more interesting
cards of each pack (usually the court cards and aces) should be
mounted so that they can be turned to for easy reference. This
can be done in a large scrap-book with dark coloured pages,
or in a large loose-leaf photograph album, or, most expensive
of all, on individual stiff black boards, obtainable at about one
shilling each through an artists' supplies store. If the scrap-
book method is used, it might be worth investing in one
scrap-book for each country or area—England, France, Italy,
Spain, Switzerland, Germany, Austria, U.S.A. (and the rest)
so that the cards of each country can be easily compared.
In any case, every collector discovers as he goes along adjust-
ments and improvements which suit his own particular
collection.

One of the most satisfactory methods of mounting cards is by
using transparent photo corners, with either white or black
backgrounds. This saves any damaging adhesive attaching
itself to the cards.

Room should be left at the top of each page or board for a
descriptive label including an index reference number. An
index card should then be completed, giving all information
known about the pack, and the same reference number put on
a piece of paper, to be attached to the remaining, unmounted
cards before they are stored away in a box or drawer. The
object of mounting cards is to display their attractiveness and
to include every card which tells one something about the pack.
For example, on an old English pack the design and wording
on the ace of spades will tell you the maker's name, the amount
of tax paid (this varied greatly from decade to decade until
1832) and, consequently, give you a good idea of the age of the
pack (see page 195). When an English pack is mounted, therefore, almost invariably the ace of spades should be included.
Sometimes a pack will contain more than the usual number of
'interesting' cards. A 'transfomation' pack (see page 164) for
instance, carries a different design on each of its cards, some

of them extremely ingenious, and requires for its display an open double page, or two boards joined together.

Indexing is quite a problem and few collectors seem to have evolved a satisfactory system. Perhaps the best method is simply to number consecutively each pack acquired, but to keep a simple cross-reference index containing makers' names, types, etc. A more complicated system keeps a series of numbers for each country (each country where the cards were *used*, that is, not necessarily where they were made). But, either way, the numbered index card should contain as much information as you have gathered about the pack, and might read as follows:

Reference Number: 43
Number of Cards in full pack: 52
Number of Cards obtained: 49
Country of Origin: Italy
Country of Use: Italy
Date: 1953
Maker's Name and Address: Dal Negro, Treviso
How obtained: On holiday in Venice 1954
Descriptive Comments:
Standard Venetian pattern. Missing cards: 4, 5, 6 of swords

The cross-reference cards might be headed 'Dal Negro, Treviso' and 'Venetian pattern', and both would refer to the master card. My own system is a good deal more complex than this, and not altogether better for it!

Closely connected with indexing is, of course, the matter of identification and dating. Modern packs bought in mint condition present little difficulty; at a pinch, the year of purchase will provide an accurate enough guide. But almost every other pack requires some greater or lesser degree of detective work to uncover origin and date. Characteristics peculiar to various countries will be dealt with in later chapters and the following are only general pointers:

1. Tax stamps. In England, Italy, Germany and Austria, these can provide useful guides to dating (see page 194).

2. Maker's name and address. These appear at least once on some card or other in most packs.

3. Backs of cards. In England and the U.S.A. decorated card backs were a mid-nineteenth-century phenomenon, having previously been plain. In other countries patterned backs have been in use far longer.

4. Rounded corners. These appeared for the first time at the end of the nineteenth century.

5. Printing processes. These can be confusing, particularly in Italy and Austria, where crudely cut and coloured wood-block printed cards persisted until the end of the nineteenth century.

Identification of cards can only be a matter of perseverance and practice. I hope the following pages may prove of use to collectors, but there can never be a complete reference book on cards, simply because it is impossible to gather the information together. Probably every collector has discovered something that no other collector is aware of, simply because, say, he discovered in his attic one day a pack of cards by a hitherto unheard-of Hungarian printer of the eighteenth century. Reference books are very few and far between, and are mostly out of print. Museums are the only answer for the serious student. I recommend particularly, if possible, a visit to the Print Room of the British Museum (a ticket must be obtained) where Lady Charlotte Schreiber's collection is housed (accumulated at the end of the nineteenth century). The catalogue of the collection (now out of print, though second-hand copies are worth hunting for) makes a fine reference book on its own, and any pack can be studied on request. The Guildhall's Phillips collection may also be studied, though it is less fine than the Schreiber. The Victoria and Albert Museum also has a somewhat smaller collection, and an excellent reference library for use of which permission must be obtained. Otherwise, I can offer only a short bibliography (see p. 202) and hope that some of the books listed may come your way. Most are likely to be expensive, but the O'Donoghue catalogue of the Schreiber collection is worth its weight in gold to the serious collector, and is not yet particularly rare.

The following chapters (Part I) attempt to give some sort of framework on which an aspiring collector may base his own individual collection. The origins of cards lie largely in Europe and it is on Europe that these pages concentrate. History shows a great deal of complicated to-ing and fro-ing of armies and territories, governments and kings, and the picture of Europe cardwise shows a number of instances where borders are new-fangled ideas which cannot affect the habits of card players. On each side of part of the borders of Germany and Austria, or of Switzerland and Italy, or of Austria and Czechoslovakia, for example, the cards used locally are the same. It is a little difficult, therefore, to give an exact picture of the boundaries of each locality, but allowing for such overlaps, the continent is divided as follows for the purpose of cataloguing its card patterns and history:

1. Italy
2. Spain and Portugal
3. France and England
4. Germany
5. The territory covered by the Austro-Hungarian Empire at 1914
6. Switzerland and the Rest.

It should be emphasized that this division is made only for the purpose of demonstrating the basic regional patterns. The succeeding chapters (Part II) deal with the fashions which developed and built on these patterns, but which spread their influence and form through several or many different countries. The universality of cards is underlined by the world-wide appeal of bridge, the continuity is emphasized by the *tarocchino* cards of Bologna, which have been used there and there alone for over five centuries.

It seems appropriate here to offer a little advice on one aspect of collecting. Where old packs of cards are concerned, do not be too fussy about completeness or even condition, unless you are extremely wealthy, or patient, or both. Even a single card from an interesting pack can be informative—and nice to have. A used card is a normal card, and unless it is positively unhygienic, should be regarded as something which has existed for the purpose for which it was created—to give entertainment. If a better specimen should eventually come along, so much the better, but to obtain a full picture of the world in cards, one cannot afford to be too particular.

PART I

The Standard Cards of Europe

CHAPTER I

Italy

ITALY today enjoys reasonable political unity, but this, of course, has not always been the case. The fourteen different regional patterns of her cards (a century ago it was fifteen) reflect the influx of French, Spanish and Imperial influences in the past as well as the struggles for identity of the individual states.

From the present-day card-collector's point of view, however, Italy is divided roughly into three parts: the people of the north and north-east using cards with purely Italian suit-marks; the southern two-thirds of the peninsula using Italo-Spanish suits and the north-west using French suits. The cards with the earliest origins come in the first category, and we must now examine the controversial subject of tarot cards, which use this system.

These cards are virtually never used in the Anglo-Saxon world except for fortune-telling. This has resulted in their being surrounded by a strange mystique and a mass of nebulous theories: that they originated as religious tablets in the temples of Ancient Egypt, that the designs are corruptions from Hebrew or cabalistic signs, that the gypsies brought them to Europe from Egypt, that they have strange powers, and so on. They are, however, still used as playing cards in several European countries (including Italy, where they originated) and there is no evidence that I can find that they were seriously used for divination before the eighteenth century. Certainly they were known as playing cards in Europe before the gypsies arrived early in the fifteenth century. There is, for instance, in the Correr Museum in Venice, a fragment of a tarot pack, hand-illuminated and made for the Visconti family, belonging to this period; others are to be found in the Bibliothèque Nationale in Paris. There is evidence that they have been used as playing cards ever since. Incidentally, when in Italy or France, the collector who is searching for tarot cards as opposed to the normal 4-suit pack should always ask for *tarocchi* or *tarots* and not *carte da giuoco* or *cartes à jouer:* presumably one plays at tarot *or* cards.

The curiosity aroused by this pack stems from certain cards peculiar to it. Basically a tarot pack has four suits which comprise four, six or ten pip cards and four court cards, king, queen, mounted knight and jack, plus twenty-two separate trump cards or, in the case of the Florentine tarot called *minchiate*, forty-one separate trumps. It is the design of these trump cards (*atutti*) which has resulted in more books being written about the significance of tarot cards than about all the rest of playing cards put together. My own theory is that these cards were either invented or popularized in the Valley of the Taro river (a tributary of the Po) which runs remarkably close to the locality where some of the earliest tarot cards are known to have existed. The hand-painted fifteenth-century packs belonging to such great families as the Sforza, Este and Visconti are all from northern Italy. Their designs are reflected, particularly that of the Visconti pack, in the modern 62-card *tarocchino* or 'little tarot' of Bologna, used only in a tiny area in and around that city. The figures pictured thereon are certainly clothed in late fourteenth-century style.

By the end of the fifteenth century, however, it was a rather different set of designs (although dealing with identical subjects) which had become more generally accepted throughout northern Italy, Switzerland, France, Austria and Germany; and this Venetian or, as it is now known, Piedmontese or Marseillaise tarot became the most widely used of the Italian-suited tarot packs. Another early, probably fifteenth-century, pack used in a limited area between Florence and Bologna was the 97-card Florentine *minchiate* with its wealth of artistic detail (even though often crudely produced) which has now vanished from the card-playing scene.

Until approximately 1750, tarot cards wherever they were used had Italian suits. For some reason, chauvinistic or otherwise, all tarot-playing countries outside Italy from that time used tarot packs with French suits and a different style of trump card either as well as—France and Switzerland—or instead of—Belgium, Germany and Austro-Hungary—the Italian-suited ones. A fuller description of this fascinating category of tarot cards can be found in the sections devoted to these countries, but it should not be forgotten that the composition of the packs (twenty-two trump cards and up to fourteen cards in each suit) is Italian in origin.

This, it is hoped, gives some idea of the rather special place held in the scheme of card-playing Europe by the three tarot packs of north and north-eastern Italy. Originally they were designed in medieval times, dealt with medieval preoccupations which governed most of medieval life and contain a good deal of medieval Christian symbolism—a common characteristic of any early European folk art.

The less controversial, non-tarot packs of the north-east which also have purely Italian suits, are three in number: the Trentine from the Trento area, the Venetian (the most widely used); and an offshoot from the same pack, the Triestine (which is still used a good way down the eastern coastline of the Adriatic). They are all known as 52-card packs although they are also issued in a 40-card form. The Venetian would appear to be the oldest form of pack although the Trentine, about which it is difficult to find any history as it was never widely used, has details of design which remind one of the Austro-Hungarian Italian-suited pack for *trappola* (see p. 99), which is accepted as having origins almost as ancient as the tarot. Trentino is an area which has frequently bounced back and forth between the Empire and Italy, and one day evidence may well come to light that there is a definite relationship between the two packs.

Some say that the Venetian pack is the first one to be found with double-headed cards. Here it should be said that there is always room for research and correction to any statement about playing cards—which adds to the pleasure of collecting. I am not entirely convinced that the date 1602 which appears on the pack in question by Gaetano Salvotti of Vicenza is not, in fact, part of the cardmaker's address. A cardmaker of the same name was making cards in the nineteenth century in Vicenza, and it is very rare to find a firm of cardmakers surviving two centuries. Single-figure Venetian cards are known until at least 1779. Apart from this one doubtful instance double-headed cards do not appear to have existed before the mid-eighteenth century.

Italo-Spanish suited cards exist south of the Po valley. The most interesting pattern used is that for the Piacentine pack which has strong links with Spain and France (see under aluette cards, page 76) and even a minor relationship with our own pack, for the Piacentine king of money and the English king of hearts originally bore the same figure. It was probably the first Spanish pack to be introduced to Italy, and the other regions evolved designs of their own at a subsequent time. The term Italo-Spanish is used here rather than Spanish, for although the suit-marks used are Spanish in design and arrangement, Italo-Spanish cards for the last two centuries clearly came from Italy for the following reasons.

From the very few packs which have survived from before 1750 it appears that Spanish-suited cards followed the Italian fashion of reinforcing the edges of cards by binding them with a layer of paper turned over from the back. And the Spanish cards were narrow like the Italian ones. It was only from inscriptions, usually barely legible, that the country of origin could be deduced. By the end of the eighteenth century, however, Spanish cards ceased to have turnover edges and introduced a practice which Italy ignored, that of making a number of breaks in the border line surrounding the design, the number being determined according to the suit of the card (none for money, one for cups, two for swords and three for clubs). Spanish cards also became broader. Italo-Spanish cards have followed a regional pattern of design which in three cases out of four (the fourth being the Piacentine pack mentioned previously) bears no relation to Spanish designs. They share with Spain the characteristic that all kings are portrayed standing, whereas in the purely Italian-suited packs, the kings are always shown enthroned. (In double-headed court cards, however, the throne usually becomes invisible.)

The Piacentine pack is used in an area which, roughly speaking, covers the length of western Italy from Piacenza and Bologna to Rome. In common with the other Italo-Spanish packs it comprises only forty cards, although its French and Spanish relations go as high as forty-eight or even fifty-two to the pack.

The Romagnole pack resembles the Piacentine in several ways but is probably much later in origin, the court figures being clothed in what appear to be eighteenth-century garments. It is used in the eastern part of the peninsula in an area between Ravenna and Rome—the area covered by the old Papal States—and is known also to be used in the same areas as the Piacentine cards.

The Neapolitan and Sicilian packs are quite different from the other two Italo-Spanish packs, probably a legacy of the days of the Kingdom of the Two Sicilies. They abandon the characteristically narrow Italian shape, and are small and squat in appearance. The court figures are always small and realistically drawn: this lack of formalized style probably betokens late origins. I have not so far been able to trace a card with these patterns which could definitely be dated earlier than 1800.

Under the heading of Italo-Spanish cards one should perhaps mention a pack used in Sardinia which is based on the designs of an early nineteenth-century Spanish pack. It is, apart from having no breaks in its frame-lines, entirely Spanish in character.

The third, and possibly least interesting, category of cards used in Italy is that with French suits. Two of these patterns, the Piedmontese and Genoese, are versions (though different ones) of the Paris pattern which, since the eighteenth century and before the triumph of universal bridge playing, had been used in one form or another in most parts of Europe. Another, the Lombard, is possibly the oldest and is shared with the Ticino district of Switzerland; and the fourth and fifth, both from Tuscany, merely demonstrate in their design the resurgence of romantic feeling prevalent in Italy during the last one hundred and fifty years: the designs are quite attractive of their kind but exist in a small cul-de-sac so far as their place in traditional card design is concerned. Both are used in the same area around Florence, and, because of their size are known as the little (*piccolo*) and large (*grande*) packs.

HOW TO IDENTIFY ITALIAN STANDARD PACKS

Piedmontese tarot (tarocco piemontese)

Italian suits. Seventy-eight cards. Four suits of 14 (ace, king, queen, knight, jack and 2–10) plus twenty-two trumps, the first twenty-one being numbered. Until about 1870 the cards were usually narrow and had turnover edges. Cards in this style with French inscriptions came from an area surrounding Bologna. In other parts of Italy, Italian inscriptions were adhered to. Modern cards usually have trumps and courts with double-headed figures (see fig. 4) and are large and broad in shape. The trumps are named as follows (although there can be infinite variety in spelling and occasionally variation in the very name). French names and usual English translations are also given. Modern trump cards have Arabic numbering, older ones had Roman figures.

No.	Italian	French	English
I	Il Bagattel	Le Bateleur	The Mountebank
II	La Papessa	La Papesse	The Popess
III	L'Imperatrice	L'Imperatrice	The Empress
IIII	L'Imperatore	L'Empereur	The Emperor
V	Il Papa	Le Pape	The Pope
VI	Gli Amanti	L'Amoureux	The Lover(s)
VII	Il Carro	Le Chariot	The Chariot
VIII	La Giustizia	La Justice	Justice
VIIII	L'Eremita	L'Ermite	The Hermit
X	Ruota della Fortuna	Roue de Fortune	Wheel of Fortune
XI	La Forza	La Force	Fortitude

No.	Italian	French	English
XII	L'Appeso	Le Pendu	The Hanging Man
XIII	La Morte or Lo Specchio or unnamed	(Unnamed)	(Death)
XIIII	La Temperanza	Temperance	Temperance
XV	Il Diavolo	Le Diable	The Devil
XVI	La Torre	La Maison de Dieu	The Tower
XVII	Le Stelle	L'Etoile	The Star(s)
XVIII	La Luna	La Lune	The Moon
XVIIII	Il Sole	Le Soleil	The Sun
XX	Il Giudizio or L'Angelo	Le Jugement	Judgement
XXI	Il Mondo	Le Monde	The World
O or XXII	Il Matto	Le Mat or Le Fol	The Fool

The maker's name is often found on one of the low pip cards of the cups or money suit. Early cardmakers referred to the sign of the place where they worked and sometimes omitted their names. Hence *Al Mondo*, *Al Cigno*, *alla Columba*, etc. (All these were Bolognese signs.)

Bolognese tarocchino cards (or *tarocco di Bologna*)

Italian suits. Sixty-two cards. Four suits of 10 (ace, king, queen, knight, jack and 6–10) plus twenty-two trumps of which only nos. 5 to 16 are numbered, in Arabic numerals. The shape is long and narrow and for over a century double-headed courts and trumps have been employed. The trumps and court cards are unnamed. Originally the trumps had subjects identical with those of the Piedmontese tarots although arranged in a different order; but somehow Bologna or its cards incurred the wrath of papal authorities and the four cards dealing with imperial and papal subjects (Emperor, Empress, Pope and Popess) were withdrawn in 1725 and four Moors or Satraps replaced them. Today the trumps are, therefore, as follows:

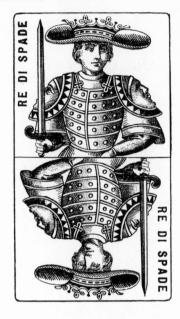

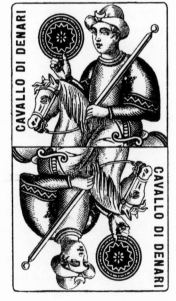

Fig. 4. Modern Piedmontese tarot cards. Compare with the same cards from a *tarocchino* pack (fig. 5) and a *minchiate* pack (fig. 6).

Unnumbered: The Mountebank, the four Moors, The Moon, The Sun, Judgement or The Angel, The World, The Fool.

Numbered: 5, The Lovers: 6, The Chariot: 7, Temperance: 8, Justice: 9, Fortitude: 10, The Wheel of Fortune: 11, The Hermit: 12, The Hanging Man: 13, Death: 14, The Devil: 15: The Tower, 16: The Star.

The designs incorporate details found on the earliest cards, such as the navigators appearing on the Moon card and a figure holding a distaff on the Sun card.

See fig. 5.

Around the beginning of the eighteenth century a highly artistic pack of *tarocchino* cards was designed by Giuseppe Maria Mitelli for the Bentivoglio family. Although the interpretation of the subjects was very imaginative and 'non-standard', the form of the pack remained constant with the customary *tarocchino*. A coarse copy of the pack was made a century later.

Florentine minchiate cards (roughly translated, *minchiate* means 'to play at trumps')

Italian suits (with variation in placement of sword pips). Ninety-seven cards. Four suits of 14 (ace, king, queen, knight, jack and 2–10) plus forty-one trumps, the first thirty-five being numbered with Roman numerals. Court cards and trumps are unnamed. The cards are on the small side but with the usual narrow Italian shape. The swords on the pip cards are straight rapiers rather than scimitars and cross each other at right angles to make a trellis-like pattern. (This phenomenon also occurs on Portuguese cards, q.v.) The knights of cups and money are shown as monsters, half-human and half-dragon, and those of swords and clubs are represented by centaurs. The jacks of swords and clubs are predictably aggressive young men (the Italian jack is a *fante*) but those of cups and money portray a young lady or *fantiglia*. The subjects of the trump cards are as follows:

I. The Mountebank, II. The Grand Duke (usually a rather effeminate figure), III. The Western Emperor, IIII. The Eastern Emperor, V. The Lovers, VI. Temperance, VII. Fortitude,

Fig. 5. Bolognese *tarocchino*
card.

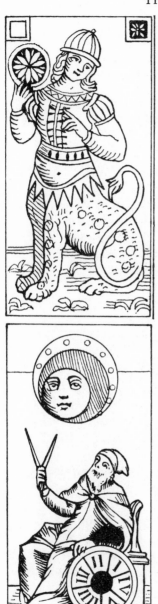

Fig. 6. Florentine *minchiate* cards. Note the characteristic monster on the knight of money card.

VIII. Justice, VIIII. The Wheel of Fortune, X. The Chariot, XI. The Hermit, XII. The Hanging Man, XIII. Death, XIIII. The Devil, XV. The Tower, XVI. Hope, XVII. Prudence, XVIII. Faith, XVIIII. Charity, XX. Fire, XXI. Water, XXII. Earth, XXIII. Air, XXIIII. The Scales, XXV. The Virgin, XXVI. The Scorpion, XXVII. The Ram, XXVIII. The Goat, XXVIIII. The Archer, XXX. The Crab, XXXI. The Fishes, XXXII. The Water-carrier, XXXIII. The Lion (starting with this card, the remainder of the trumps, except the Fool have bright red backgrounds and are *Arie* cards), XXXIIII. The Bull, XXXV. The Twins. Then follow the unnumbered cards: The Star, The Moon, The Sun, The Angel (who floats above the city of Florence), The World and The Fool.

The trump cards and court cards are invariably shown with single figures and no double-headed version is known to me. The cards have fallen out of use and no Florentine I have met has ever heard of them. So far as I can make out, the last pack to be made was by Solesio of Genoa in 1890. The maker's name very rarely appears on *minchiate* cards, but at least 90 per cent of such cards come from Florence or Bologna. See fig. 6.

The Venetian pattern (*Venete* or *Trevisane telate*)

Italian suits. Forty or fifty-two cards. Four suits of 10 or 13 (ace, king, knight, jack and 2–7 or 2–10). Narrow Italian shape. Court cards have been double-headed for over a century at least.

Distinctive cards: All aces carry punning or humorous mottoes which appear to be constant although the spelling varies. On the ace of cups PER UN PUNTO MARTIN PERSE LA CAPPA, on the ace of swords NON TI FIDAR DI ME SE IL CUOR TI MANCA, on the ace of money NON VAL SAPER A CHI HA FORTUNA CONTRA, and on the ace of clubs SE TI PERDI TUO DANO. The jack of swords holds an executioner's sword point down in his right hand, and a severed head in his left. Court cards are unnamed.

These cards were probably known in many places outside

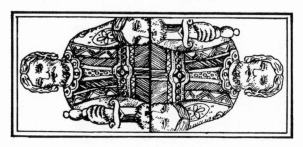

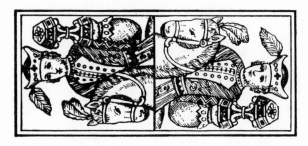

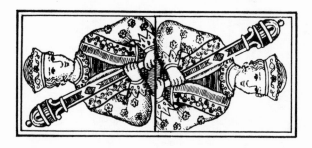

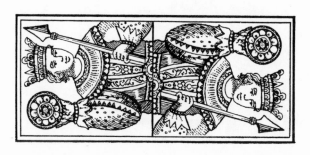

Fig. 7. Venetian pattern with double-headed court cards. Note the executioner jack of swords. Compare with the same cards from the Triestine pack (fig. 8) and the Trentine pack (fig. 9).

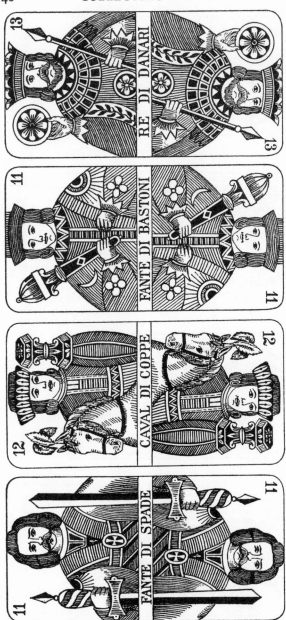

Fig. 8. Triestine pattern: note the characteristic labels on the court cards.

the area immediately surrounding Venice and may well have
been introduced to many foreign ports by Venetian sailors—
there is even an Italian-suited 52-card pack with Greek mottoes
known to have been made in Corfu earlier this century.
    See fig. 7.

The Triestine pattern (*Triestine telate*)

    Italian suits. Forty or fifty-two cards. Four suits of 10 or 13
(ace, king, knight, jack and 2–7 or 2–10). Narrow Italian shape.
Clearly an offshoot of the Venetian pack but with its own
characteristics. I have only seen packs with double-headed
courts although earlier ones may well exist. Court cards are all
named with label at centre of card, RE DI COPPE, CAVAL DI
DANARI, FANTE DI BASTONI, etc.
    Apart from the named courts, the mottoes on the distinctive
aces, although different from their Venetian neighbours', are
the chief identifying characteristic. On the ace of cups UNA
COPPA DI BUON VIN FA CORRAGIO E FA MOR BIN is usual. On the
other aces the mottoes have not remained constant, but those
used today are often IL GIUOCO DELLA SPADA A MOLTI NON
AGGRADA on the ace of spades, and MOLTE VOLTE LE GIUOCATE
VAN FINIRE ABASTONATE on the ace of clubs. The Italian tax
stamp usually takes up the main part of the ace of money.
    See fig. 8.

The Trentine pattern (*Trentine telate*)

    Italian suits. Forty or fifty-two cards. Four suits of 10 or 13
(ace, king, knight, jack and 2–7 or 2–10). Narrow Italian shape.
Known single-figure even today, but also double-headed.
    Distinctive cards: Standing in or on the ace of cups is a
winged cupid with bow and arrow. The knights are all bareheaded. A dog leaps up beside the jack of cups. There are no
mottoes on the aces. See fig. 9.

The Piacentine pattern (*Piacentine telate*)

    Italo-Spanish suits. Forty cards. Four suits of 10 cards (ace,
king, knight, jack and 2–7). Narrow Italian shape (French and

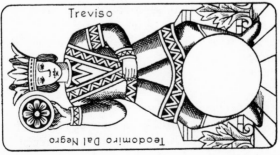
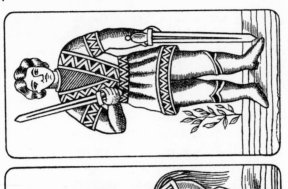

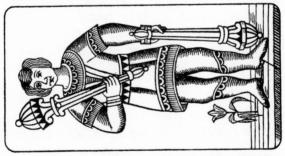
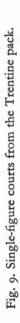

Fig. 9. Single-figure courts from the Trentine pack.

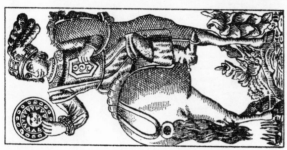

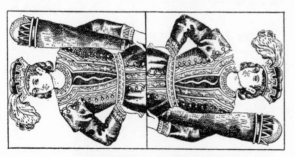

Fig. 10. The Piacentine pattern. Two jacks from a pack with double-headed courts, and a king and knight of money from one with single-figure court cards: note the knight of money's distinctive pattern.

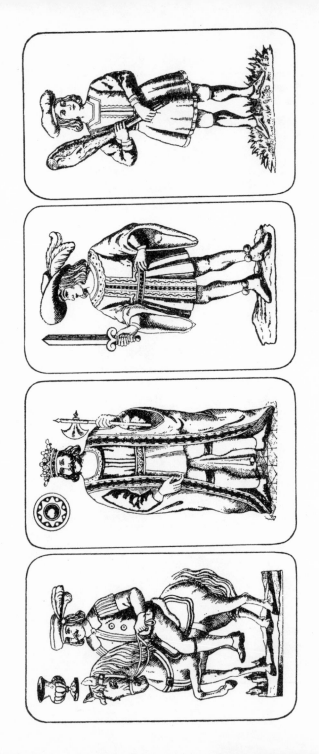

Fig. 11. The Romagnole pattern. The jack of swords is a useful aid to identification of this pack.

Spanish versions of the pack are, except for very early cards, much broader). Known single and double-headed even today.

Distinctive cards: The ace of money, when not entirely devoted to tax stamps, shows a single-headed, crowned eagle (as opposed to the Neapolitan double-headed eagle and the uncrowned single-headed eagle of Sicily). The king of money holds an axe. The jack of cups holds a halberd and wears a sword. The knight of money is on a horse which has its back to the viewer, so that the rider has to twist round in his saddle to present his suit-mark to the world. On old packs the centre coin of the five of money contains the heads in profile of a facing man and woman. The clothing worn by the court figures is medieval in appearance.

See fig. 10.

The Romagnole pattern (*Romagnole telate*)

Italo-Spanish suits. Composition as for the Piacentine pack, to which it is clearly related (marks in common include a cherub on the ace of swords and an axe-carrying king of money). I have never found a double-headed version of this pack. Clothing on the courts appears to come from a later age than the Piacentine, probably the eighteenth century.

Distinctive cards: The axe-carrying king of cups. The jacks of cups and money both wear baggy trousers. The jack of swords wears a large befeathered cavalier hat. See fig. 11.

The Neapolitan pattern (*Napoletane* or *Baresi telate*)

Italo-Spanish suits. Forty cards. Four suits of 10 (ace, king, knight, jack and 2–7). Broad and squat and small (approx. 3 in. by 2 in.) in appearance. The courts of each suit stand on a different coloured platform: red for cups, blue for swords, yellow for money and green for clubs. Always single-figure courts.

Distinctive cards: The ace of money with its double-headed eagle. The courts on platforms. The jack of swords holding his weapon point downward and a branch in his right hand. A gargoyle face glares out at the join of the 3 of clubs.

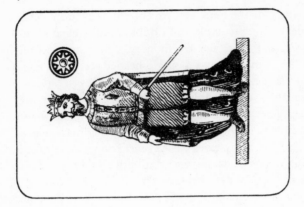

Fig. 12A. The Neapolitan pattern: note the 'platforms' described on page 45.

Crudity of wood-block production of Neapolitan cards does not necessarily mean great age: this form of printing was used up till about 1890 and the blocks were used until nothing but a faint blur appeared on many of the cards. See figs. 12A and 12B.

The Sicilian pattern (Siciliane telate)

Italo-Spanish suits. Same composition as for the Neapolitan

Fig. 12B. The Neapolitan pattern.

pack. Also small and squat in appearance. Always single-figure courts. Many courts among the jacks and knights have bare arms, possibly a tribute to the Sicilian sun. Each court value stands on different coloured plot—the kings on green, the knights on yellow and the jacks on red.

Distinctive cards: Many of the low value pip cards have vignettes on them, e.g. a small fish on the two of cups, a puppy on the two of swords, a cottage on the ace of swords. The

Fig. 13. The Sicilian pattern. The style is similar to the Neapolitan pattern (figs. 12A and 12B), but detail of design is quite different.

single-headed eagle appears on the ace of money. See fig. 13.

Florentine pattern (*carte Fiorentine grandi*)

French suits. Usually forty cards. Four suits of 10 (ace, king, queen, jack and 2–7). This large-format Florentine or Tuscan pack probably evolved some time during the last century. Court figures are realistically drawn without formalized style, and are dressed in Renaissance costumes.

Distinctive cards: The jack of clubs carries a large book. The queen of hearts carries a letter. The king of hearts stands by a table on which rests a large document with a seal attached. The jack of spades holds a shield in one hand, the other resting on the hilt of his sword.

See fig. 14.

Tuscan pattern (*carte Toscane, formato piccolo*)

French suits. Usually forty cards. Same composition as other Florentine or Tuscan pack. This smaller-format pack probably has its origins in the same period as its larger neighbour. The figures on the courts are similar in style but differ entirely in detail. Single-figure courts only are used.

Distinctive cards: The jack of hearts, dressed in Venetian Renaissance costume, holds an arrow in his left hand. The jack of spades carries a small spear. Each king holds a short baton. The queens are obviously not royal.

See fig. 15.

The Lombard or Milanese pattern (*Milanesi telate*)

French suits. Forty or fifty-two cards. Same composition as other French-suited packs. This pattern is also used in Italian Switzerland which, until 1803, was part of the Duchy of Milan: even after that date Milan exercised a good deal of influence over the new canton of Ticino. The cards of the two areas are indistinguishable save for maker's name or place of origin. The design of the cards is reminiscent of several used in eighteenth-century south and south-eastern France and may well be related. There is ample room for research here: the main

Fig. 14. The Florentine
pattern, referred to as the
'large' style when compared
with the smaller Tuscan pack
(see Fig. 15). The jack of
hearts is shown here with the
suit-mark omitted.

Fig. 15. The 'small' Tuscan pattern: the jack of hearts is shown with suit-mark omitted.

problem is to find early material with which to make comparisons. The shape, however, has narrow, Italian proportions.

Distinctive cards: The badge of Milan appears on the chest of the jack of clubs (the upper half of a human body protrudes from the mouth of a crowned serpentine monster). A falcon or parrot perches on the hand of the king of diamonds, and the king of spades appears in profile with his sceptre resting against his shoulder.

Nowadays these cards are invariably found with double-headed courts. Early packs are known with single figures, and also Italian-style turnover edges.

See fig. 16.

Piedmontese pattern (*Piemontesi telate*)

French suits. Forty or fifty-two cards. Same composition as other French-suited packs. This is a straightforward adaptation of the French Paris-pattern pack—varieties of which are known all over Europe. A fuller description of that pack will be found on p. 62 but, unlike the French version, the double-headed courts of modern Piedmontese packs are divided in two by a horizontal line instead of a diagonal one. This characteristic also distinguishes Piedmontese from Genoese cards. Single-figure courts, however, must have a maker's name or other mark of identity to ensure that they are Italian in origin. In fact, both the Italian packs are hard to identify with certainty unless such marks are apparent on the case or the cards themselves.

The Genoese pattern (*Genovesi telate*)

French suits. Forty or fifty-two cards. Same composition as other French-suited packs. This pack is clearly the result of some period of French occupation, for its design is purely Parisian, although the colouring is green, gold, red and black instead of the more usual French blue, red and yellow. Unfortunately Belgium has taken the same variation of the French cards for general use, so a maker's name, etc., is essential for positive identification.

Fig. 16. The Lombard or Milanese pattern. The king of diamonds (suit-mark omitted) carries a bird found on eighteenth century French cards: the badge of Milan appears on the jack of clubs.

The problem of dating cards is always a headache for the collector, particularly as one must invariably rely on one's own knowledge and judgement. As regards Italy, the problem is complicated by the fact that, of all card players throughout the world, the Italians are by far the most violent, and a pack of modern cards can have an almost antique appearance at the end of a short train journey. Also, Italian cardmakers used the old method of wood-block printing right up to the end of the last century, a process which, when combined with crude methods of colouring by stencil or hand, makes cards look older than they are.

Tax stamps can be helpful here: they are dealt with a little more fully in Chapter XI but here it might be said that any Italian card with a stamp on its ace of money or hearts including in its legend REGNO D'ITALIA (Kingdom of Italy) belongs to a period after 1862. (Prior to 1862 individual territories used their own stamps.) After the Second World War, of course, this legend became REPUBBLICA ITALIANA. In some instances, due to territorial exchanges, apparently foreign tax stamps appeared on Italian cards (such as Austrian stamps on Venetian packs) but these are special cases which can usually be explained by quick reference to a history book.

CHAPTER II

Spain and Portugal

I HAVE already spoken in the chapter on Italian cards of the characteristics of Spanish-suited cards and mentioned their strong influence on the design of both Italian and French cards. So far as I can tell, the earliest surviving examples of Spanish-suited cards were actually made in France (Toulouse) at the end of the fifteenth century, and they were also made in Paris only a few years later. Henry d'Allemagne, in fact, suggests that the Spaniards took their cards from Flanders: others believe that the Moors introduced them in the fourteenth century. Whatever their origins, Spanish cards had settled down with their own characteristics by the end of the sixteenth century. The Spanish word for Spanish-suited cards is *'naipes'*—possibly derived from the 'Saracenic' word for chance—*naib*—or the Flemish word for paper—*knaep*. The Spanish word for French-suited cards (rarely used before this century) is *barajas*.

The principal standard pattern used in the early days is more fully described under *aluette* cards in the French section, as the cards are still used in France, though not in Spain. They bear as the centre coin on the 5 of money portraits of a facing king and queen, probably taken from a coin of the time of Ferdinand and Isabella (late fifteenth century). The name of the reigning monarch was usually found on the ace of money. Paradoxically, by the middle of the eighteenth century these cards were widely used in France and Italy but had almost disappeared in Spain. From then onwards no set pattern lasted more than a few years (except that in the south the knight of cups usually bore the legend AHI VA) although the standing kings and the traditional positioning and shape of the suit-marks were scrupulously observed. The breaks in the border lines, originating at the end of the eighteenth century, are still employed (one of cups, two for swords, three for clubs and none for money).

Spanish-suited cards travelled with colonization, and are still used in south and central America; all are clearly Spanish in origin but each has its own design.

Portugal today plays with French-suited cards but once upon a time originated or at least disseminated one of the most fascinating packs ever issued. It is a will-o'-the-wisp pack, and every time I come across it, it has come from a different part of the world. It comprises forty-eight cards of four Spanish suits: king, queen, knight and ace–9. The aces each bear a dragon. The swords and clubs are straight but crossed in a trellis design (rather like those of the Florentine *minchiate*). A male figure entwines himself round the two crossed clubs in some packs: this card sometimes gives rise to the idea that the pack contains four court cards.

The earliest of these packs that I have seen was made by Pietro Ciliberto of no stated address in 1597. Another, but altogether anonymous pack, is dated 1610. In 1694 a Portuguese pack was made by Infirrera which has survived. In the eighteenth century an Indian pack (on small pieces of lacquered paper) appeared with the Spanish suits and dragons on the aces. Back in Europe, another anonymous pack has survived from the early nineteenth century. Later in the same century the pack turns up in Brazil described as being Portuguese. Recently a collector showed me some very crudely produced hand-painted cards which someone had brought to him from the East Indies: the suit-marks and dragons, and the correct order of court cards, were all evident. There is a pack still in use in Japan today 'borrowed from sixteenth-century Portuguese adventurers' and now called The Winter Cherry on which the familiar characteristics can be seen.

This pack is a good example of the way in which history is reflected in playing cards.

CHAPTER III

France and England

THE WEALTH and complexity of playing cards and their history in France can be illustrated by the fact that in 1906 an enormous two-volume work was published dealing almost exclusively with the subject.[1] Some statistics on cardmaking in France seem quite overwhelming: in 1754, in one province alone, over 200,000 packs were made; the number of master cardmakers alone runs into thousands; cards were subjected to every possible wind of political change and, indeed, put to a great number of purposes. When one grew tired of playing with the cards they might become scrap paper on which to write accounts or invitations, business cards or aids in grammar lessons.

It is therefore rather sad that old cards made in France are becoming very hard to find, and also that it is the one country that I know where efforts are made to forge (albeit crudely) antique playing cards. Usually it is the appearance of the paper on which these spurious articles are printed which give them away—it is either coarse or very smooth and thin. A few genuine reprints of cards have been taken from old plates, such as the *Jeu des drapeaux*, and are well worth having, provided that they are not sold to you as originals.

The number of standard packs of cards used in France today has shrunk from the eighteenth-century thirteen or so to a mere five. The French-suited pack is the most widely used, and the one that is most often on sale. This is the sole survivor of the ten or eleven provincial packs belonging to the pre-

[1] *Les Cartes à Jouer du XIVme au XXme Siècle*, by Henry-René D'Allemagne. Hachette. Now a great rarity.

Revolutionary era. It is a rather devitalized version of the old Paris pattern and its history indicates the power as well as the conservatism of card players.

When the Revolution came, among other rather more drastic excesses, cardmakers hastened, sometimes urged on by local authorities, to remove all manner of royal insignia from the blocks used for making cards. This resulted in some fascinating and extremely rare cards with extraordinary designs. Sometimes, kings would be found with topless heads; on other cards a Phrygian cap would be painted in. Then came the time when cardmakers were no longer required to follow set patterns (to facilitate collection of taxes, each province had been required from the beginning of the eighteenth century to use a single pattern of cards) and new titles and forms were given to cards. Court cards became *Génies*, *Libertés* and *Egalités*, or *Eléments*, *Saisons* and *Cultivateurs*, or *Sages*, *Vertus* and *Braves* in place of mere kings, queens and jacks. Finally Napoleon decided that one pattern should be used throughout France, preferably with a design which would uphold the glory of himself and his Empire. Such a pack was designed by the artist David and showed Napoleon dressed as Julius Caesar as the king of diamonds. This was issued in 1810 and a similar one appeared in the following year but neither was a success. Napoleon, ever sensitive to ridicule or criticism, gave up the unequal struggle and in 1813 the revived Paris pattern, redrawn by Gatteaux, became the official French pack. The first issues of this pack show the jack of clubs carrying a shield on which is inscribed ADMINIST. DES DROITS REUNIS 1813 and in the centre of the shield, in minute lettering, GATTEAUX. The next date found on the shield is 1816. There is very little change in the basic design but in some instances the 1813 cards show an imperial eagle on the king of hearts' robes which, in 1816 (but only in some instances) becomes a fleur-de-lis pattern. There was no change apparent until a new date, 1827, appeared on the shield although by this time double-headed courts had arrived on the card-playing scene. Later the date 1853 was used. Finally, towards the end of the century, the dated shield disappeared and was replaced by a number of different devices varying according to the maker.

French court cards are usually named. This has always been so in the Paris area although the practice was infrequent in the provinces. Today packs are found both with and without these names which are given on page 64.

The actual design of the court cards of the Paris pattern probably belongs to the fifteenth century. It would appear that throughout France the figures on court cards were taken from a sort of 'pool', for in several regions the same figure appears on cards although probably in a different suit. For instance, the king with a falcon on his hand appears as the king of clubs in Auvergne, as the king of hearts in Lyons, the king of diamonds in Dauphiné, the king of hearts in Provence and do not forget that there is the remotely connected character in Milan, the king of diamonds who also carries a bird on his hand. Another repeating figure is the axe-brandishing king of money found in the Piacentine pack in Italy; he is known as the king of clubs in Provence, the king of spades in Languedoc, the king of money again in Brittany and the king of hearts in England, as well as in an early Rouen pack and an Antwerp pack from which our cards may have developed. There is a possibility that these figures, like so many subjects of early popular art, derived from the saints and legendary heroes. I have not yet discovered a likely identity for the king with the falcon, but I have found several examples of early woodcut portraits of St Matthew with an axe.

As I have mentioned, at the beginning of the eighteenth century the tax inspectors of the various regions caused a set pattern to be used in each region. These patterns are described later but the designs of the cards used in these packs often go back a good many hundreds of years. It is impossible, however, to give much idea of the standard patterns in the very early days apart from one or two areas (notably Rouen and Lyons) and as the matter is of academic interest only, notes on such patterns are necessarily rather sketchy.

Another standard pattern still in use in France but rarely

found outside Brittany is the *aluette* pack which has Spanish
suit-marks (although today it does not have breaks in the
border round the central design). At first glance the pack would
seem to be a regional oddity, quite unconnected with the outside world. Its female cavaliers are, as far as I know, a unique
feature, and at first the decoration of some of the pip cards
makes the pack look quite unlike anything else. However, a
little research indicates that this form of the pack is unknown
before the 1770s: prior to that date it was less startling and
florid in appearance although containing many of the same
features, and was used in parts of south-western France and
northern Spain; it was also the pattern of card which crossed
from the Iberian to the Italian peninsula and became the
Piacentine pack. The female cavaliers were not included in the
earlier packs, but the 5 of money with facing heads was, and
these heads were most probably those of Ferdinand and
Isabella of Spain. This places the origins of the pack in the
late fifteenth century and indeed there are cards of that period
from Toulouse with Spanish suit-marks which would seem to
confirm this. The date 1587 appears on the earliest pack I have
been able to find which is undoubtedly *aluette* although the
cardmakers of both Toulouse and Limoges, both of which
traded considerably with Spain, made packs of cards with
Spanish suit-marks for a hundred years at least before that, and
in fifteenth-century Toulouse cardmakers were termed '*naiperii*'
from the Spanish word for makers of Spanish-suited cards,
rather than '*carterii*' which they later became.

Aluette was a game known to Rabelais, and one can
appreciate its appeal to this rather rumbustious character from
the fact that it involves as much cheating as possible. I have
never seen it being played but I understand that the most
efficient deceiver is accorded the doubtful compliment of
being the most skillful player. The game is still played in
Brittany.

Another Spanish-suited pack still currently used in France
is the Catalan pack. It is used only in a small corner of south-
west France and is unlike anything else. I have not so far traced

it back for more than about a hundred and forty years, but I imagine it may belong to a century before that.

The tarot pack is the only Italian-suited pack used in France —principally along the eastern borders of the country and along the south-eastern coast—although Paris cardmakers have always made a number of them. This is generally termed the *Tarot de Marseille* although other early packs are known to have originated in such distant places as Dijon, Strasbourg, Lyons, Besançon and so on. Like the *tarocchino* of Bologna, French tarot cards have in their time been subject to outside pressures; in Besançon, the Pope and Popess were replaced by Juno and Jupiter and in Strasbourg, during the Revolution, Grandfather and Grandmother took the place of the Emperor and Empress on the trump cards; otherwise they have always remained fairly constant in pattern. Their use is becoming more and more restricted to the older generation as newer pleasures and the eternal bridge and canasta take over. A further contribution to their downfall is the last of the standard packs still available in France, the French-suited tarot pack which seems to be used still in the north-east of France. This pack has a design which is shared with Germany, Switzerland and Austria, and is therefore difficult to identify unless a maker's name is in evidence.

Before moving on to a more detailed description of the composition of French packs, I must mention a pattern which is closely connected with France: that of English cards—I say English rather than British advisedly, as they were known in England long before the Union. There is, inevitably, on the meagre evidence available, a degree of uncertainty as to whether the English pattern came from Rouen, or whether the second pattern known in Rouen came from England, where the pack might well have been introduced at some time during the wars of the fifteenth century. During this period, the English also had close connections with Guienne and Gascony, many of whose old cards bear quite a resemblance to the English (or Rouen) pattern. One can only give such facts as are available. So far as I know the earliest cards which bore the English pattern were made in Antwerp in 1543 by Jehan Henault, and

the next earliest, in about 1567, by Pierre Maréchal of Rouen.
Then, at the end of the sixteenth century there was a considerable exodus of Rouen cardmakers to England. Cards were
probably known in England itself about a century before
this, for early in Edward IV's reign their import was stopped.
We probably have Oliver Cromwell to thank for the lack of
evidence on the English side of the Channel regarding early
cards; virtually no cards from before 1650 have survived the
Puritan drive against so-called frivolity, and the standard ones
that have survived are very fragmentary. They seem to be
rather smaller in format than their successors. Whatever the
exact origins of English cards may be, they clearly came some-
time from some part of France, and have many cards in
common with early French standard packs: the same pack was
used in Rouen well into the eighteenth century. It is frequently
claimed that the king of hearts is a portrait of Henry VIII but
it seems unlikely that this figure (although wielding an axe)
would appear on contemporary cards or in so many different
packs throughout France and Spain. The clothing of the figures
on the court cards suggests that the general pattern of the pack
originated in the late fifteenth century.

So much for generalities: there is clearly a great deal of
research to be done regarding the identities of the figures
appearing on both French and English cards. Who is the lamb-
carrying queen, the falcon-bearing king or the pipe-smoking
jack?

All French-suited packs are known with fifty-two or thirty-
two cards, and some with thirty-six.

The Paris pattern (Portrait de Paris)

This pattern was first firmly established as such in the middle
of the seventeenth century (based, perhaps, on the cards of
Hector of Troyes) but many of the figures thereon are known
on much earlier cards. To begin with, these cards were made in
an area surrounding Paris to an extent of about 100 to 150 miles.
In the middle of the eighteenth century, legislation was introduced making this the official *portrait* or pattern for the whole

Fig. 17. The Paris pattern as it was in the eighteenth century. These cards in modified forms appear in many different parts of Europe. The modern French version is double-headed.

of northern France. It is an easily identifiable pack although many of the early cards are crudely printed, often from worn wood-blocks. The court cards are usually named but the exact reason for, or origins of, these names are in several instances open to debate.

King of hearts (Charles). Holds an imperial orb in one hand (topped by the Cross of Lorraine) and a sword in the other. He is generally accepted as being Charlemagne. *Queen of hearts (Judic). Jack of hearts (Lahire). King of spades (David);* his right hand rests on a harp and, therefore, this figure probably represents the Biblical David. *Queen of spades (Pallas). Jack of spades (Hogier)*; a dog jumps up beside this figure; compare the jack of cups in the Italian Trentine pattern. *King of diamonds (Cézar;)* this figure is shown in profile and usually has a long nose, possibly a deliberate representation of the traditional association of the Jews with money; this nose is often particularly noticeable in German versions of this pattern and also on early English packs where the king of diamonds has the same figure.) *Queen of diamonds (Rachel). Jack of diamonds (Hector). King of clubs (Alexandre);* merely holds a sceptre in his right hand. *Queen of clubs (Argine);* holds a fan in her left hand. All the other queens hold flowers. *Jack of clubs (Lancelot);* the maker's name and trademark (if any) usually appear on this card.

Paris pattern cards had single-figure courts until about 1827 when the double-headed version came into general use.

See fig. 17.

English pattern; and Rouen pattern (Portrait de Rouen) as used until the mid-eighteenth century

As previously mentioned, it is difficult to know where the border between Rouen and England belongs. The modern English pack is obviously familiar to readers, but in several

---

P. I. Some varieties of style and content which collectors can look for. *Top:* a transformation ace of hearts, a Viennese piquet card (c. 1830), and a copper-engraved card from a pack of proverbs (c. 1700). *Centre:* Chinese coins and domino cards, and three historical figures. *Below:* an American tobacco card, an 18th-century German card, and a mystery—probably a Belgian card (c. 1810).

Plate II

cards time and frequent redrawing have obscured much original detail. The following descriptions therefore relate more to earlier cards made before the watered-down twentieth-century versions.

King of hearts; he now wields a sword handle, but this was originally a raised axe—this is one of the figures found in many parts of France. *Jack of hearts;* shown in profile, he is stepping forward with one hand holding a halberd behind his back. Originally his other hand was probably resting on his sword hilt, but this gradually became so distorted that now he appears to be clutching some indeterminate leaf. *King of spades;* holds an upright sword (q.v. Italian word for sword = *spada*). *Queen of spades;* she is the only queen to hold a sceptre—all the others merely clutch flowers. *Jack of spades;* stands in rather similar fashion to the jack of hearts but holds his halberd before him. *King of diamonds;* stands in profile, and is similar to Paris king of diamonds. *Jack of diamonds;* this figure, facing forward, wears knee-length breeches which look feathery but probably represent chain mail. He wears a sword and carries a halberd. *King of clubs;* this figure was originally the same one as that appearing on the Paris king of hearts—holding a sword and the imperial orb topped with the Cross of Lorraine. By about 1780, however, chauvinism in England had displaced the French cross, and since that time the orb has been surmounted with a nondescript leafy-looking affair. *Jack of clubs;* this jack also appears front face and holds a long arrow-like spear of a type often found in early French miniatures or illuminations depicting hunting.

English pattern cards remained single-figured on the courts until shortly after 1850; even then it was at least ten years before the more sedate London clubs would accept double-headed cards. The pattern gradually spread all over the world,

---

P. II. *Top and centre left:* Spanish (c. 1735) and French (1665) editions of Brianville's heraldic cards. *Top right:* reproduction of fifteenth-century German 6 of pomegranates. *Lower row, from left:* satirical Dutch 'Mississippi Bubble' card of 1720; 6 of swords from Albrizzi's *History of the Popes* (c. 1779); ace of spades from Lenthall's fortune-telling pack—note the tax stamp of about 1715.

Fig. 18. The English pattern as it was in the eighteenth and nineteenth centuries. Double-headed cards were introduced in about 1850.

mainly as a result of the growth of English-speaking nations. At first cards were exported to America and Australia from England, but it was not long before cardmakers in other lands set up their own presses and blocks. See fig. 18 and plate I.

The first Rouen pattern

This is a pattern of extreme rarity and its history is rather obscure. Examples made in Rouen are known from the mid-sixteenth and mid-seventeenth centuries: a further pack came from Brussels one hundred years later, and two Swedish makers produced packs at the end of the seventeenth century. The cards are long and narrow: their chief distinguishing feature is the naming of the jacks; hearts = *Siprien Roman*, that of spades has maker's name; diamonds = *Capitan Fily*, clubs = *Capitaine taillant* or *Millan*; the queens (in the same order) are *Hélène*, *Bersabée*, *Thérèse* and *Pentaxlée*; the kings are *Jullius Cézar*, *David*, *Charles* and *Hector*. The king of diamonds (Charles) is the same figure as that on the Paris king of hearts and the English king of clubs. (The actual spelling on the court cards varies from pack to pack.)

This pattern, which should not perhaps carry such a localized title as Rouennais, seems to have been completely ousted by the English-cum-Rouen pattern when the laws of 1701 demanded a single official pattern.

The Lorraine pattern, which is identical with the Burgundian pattern (*Portrait de Lorraine* and *Portrait de Bourgogne*)

These two packs are also extremely rare, particularly that originating in Lorraine which was replaced by the Paris pattern as early as 1751. The pattern followed was one which was originated by early Lyons cardmakers for cards for export to Flanders, Burgundy and Lorraine, and then adopted by cardmakers in the two areas. It is only very exceptionally that one can tell the two packs apart unless a maker's name and address is found. The most distinctive card in the pack is undoubtedly the jack of clubs who wears a helmet with a long heavy plume. This figure appears nowhere else in the French card world. The

Fig. 19. The Lyonnais pattern of the eighteenth century.

queen of diamonds wears curiously squared fur sleeves tipped with ermine—she is known elsewhere, but in Provence she is also the queen of diamonds. The kings are noteworthy for their lack of distinguishing detail; hearts carries a sceptre resting over his shoulder, spades holds what might be a scroll, diamonds holds nothing and clubs carries a short upright sceptre. On plate I is shown the characteristic jack of clubs, but unfortunately the wrong suit-mark has been stencilled on to the card.

The Lyons pattern (*Portrait de Lyon*)

There are two patterns for Lyonnais cards; the one in use until the end of the seventeenth century and the one used from the beginning of the eighteenth century up to the time of the Revolution. The first is so rare that a description seems superfluous but the square-sleeved queen turns up as the queen of clubs, the queen of hearts holds a sceptre and the jack of hearts holds a standard. This pack, oddly enough, turned up in the Swiss Vaud in the nineteenth century but I have not yet been able to find out whether this was a deliberate reproduction or whether it was in steady traditional use. It is still found, in a double-headed version, as the standard Austrian French-suited pack, which is curious since the pattern has not been used in its own country for over two hundred and fifty years.

The second pattern was widely used throughout the eighteenth century, and, apart from the Paris pattern, has left more survivors than any other regional pattern of the period. It is easily recognizable by its pipe-smoking jack of spades. The king of hearts carries a hawk on his wrist, the king of clubs carries an orb and sceptre, all the queens carry fans and flowers and the jack of clubs carries a shield. See fig. 19.

The Auvergne pattern (*Portrait d'Auvergne*)

Thiers in Auvergne has been a cardmaking centre for many centuries, and this pattern is one of the oldest in France. It shares with the Paris pattern an orb and sword-carrying king of hearts—sometimes called Charles—but otherwise is quite

Fig. 20. The pre-Revolutionary Auvergne pattern.

Fig. 21. The Languedoc
pattern which, in its larger
form, was also used in
Guienne.

distinctive. Its neighbour, Limousin, has the same pattern, except for the jack of diamonds and the jack of clubs. The king of clubs has a falcon on his wrist, the queen of spades cradles a small creature in her arm, the jacks have distinctively plumed helmets: they are all four similar in appearance, but those of hearts and spades face to their right and those of diamonds and clubs face to their left. In Limousin packs, the jacks all face in the same direction—to their right.

See fig. 20 and plate I.

The Limousin pattern (see under Auvergne, above)

The Dauphiné pattern (*Portrait de Dauphiné*)

This pattern probably originated in the sixteenth century and was used until the Revolution. I understand that no complete pack of this pattern is known to exist although millions of packs were made. I count myself lucky, therefore, to have even eight court cards from one pack in my collection. Blocks of whole sets of courts, however, have survived, enabling one to reconstruct the form of the pack. The king of diamonds has a falcon on his wrist, the king of clubs carries an orb and sword (the same figure as in some other packs), the jack of clubs stands front face, one hand on hip, the other on the top of his halberd and he wears knee-length, usually chain-mail, trousers, and a heavy sword. This figure appears in several packs in southern France, and also occurs on the Spanish-suited *aluettes* as the jack of cups. The jack of hearts and diamonds, however, are both unique and possibly display a north Italian influence in their style of dress. The jack of hearts stands with drawn sword held in his right hand while his left forefinger points up to heaven: he wears a Phrygian type of cap but otherwise seems to be dressed as a Roman soldier. The jack of diamonds, wrapped in a cloak strides forward, bareheaded—his boots have human faces on the shins.

The Provence pattern (*Portrait de Provence*)

This is another pattern with ancient origins (late fifteenth

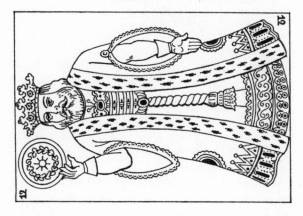

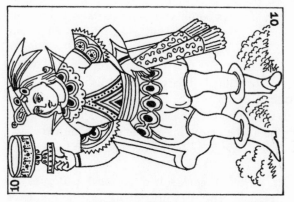

Fig. 22. The Spanish-suited Catalan pattern.

century), and contains several familiar figures. The king of hearts has a falcon on his wrist, the king of clubs wields an axe, the queen of diamonds has squared sleeves, and the jack of hearts stands with one hand on his hip, and the other hand on his halberd. The pattern was in use until the Revolution. Very early examples of the pack show the queen of hearts as a fur-covered 'wild woman'.

The Languedoc pattern and the Guienne pattern (Portrait de Languedoc and Portrait de Guienne)

Although the detail of design of these patterns is identical, they are distinguishable by the size of the cards, those from the Languedoc being considerably smaller than those from Guienne. Several figures familiar in other parts of France and England occur on these cards: the axe-wielding king here represents the spade suit; the harp is found on the king of hearts' card; the jack of spades has hand on hip and wears knee-length mail or quilted trousers; the English jack of spades is here the jack of hearts and the English jack of hearts can be recognized in the figure on the jack of clubs. The pattern was certainly known at the beginning of the seventeenth century, and was in use until the Revolution. See fig. 21 and plate I.

The heyday of the French-suited regional patterns was undoubtedly the eighteenth century: nowadays the hundreds of towns in France which once boasted any number of card-makers has dwindled and at least 90 per cent of all card production today takes place in Paris. This even applies to cards used in districts a long way from Paris, such as the Spanish- and Italian-suited patterns.

The Catalan pattern

These Spanish-suited cards are used in a very small area in south-west France and are characteristically Spanish in design, even to the line-breaks on the borders of the cards. Figure 22 gives some idea of the rather vapid design, and the most distinctive figure on the courts is the jack of money who holds

Fig. 23. Cards from a modern
Breton *aluette* pack. Note the
female 'knight' and characteristic 2 of clubs.

a French hunting horn in his left hand. There are forty-eight cards in the pack and each suit is nowadays numbered 1–12, there being no tens, and the courts being numbered 10–12.

The aluette cards of Brittany

A description of this pack and its history has already been given on page 60. It seems appropriate to give a description of the pack as used in Brittany for the last one and three-quarter centuries, as well as the earlier form which seems to have been widely used all down the western side of France.

The first pack of the modern *aluette* cards would appear to have been made in 1776 by Pierre Sigogne of Nantes who, probably as a pun on his name, incorporated the feature of storks on the 3 of cups and the ace of swords. The 2 of cups is a highly distinctive card, showing the two cups floating above a large cow lying down in a field (this card is appropriately named *la vache*): it is an interesting point that in a Spanish-suited pack made in about 1510 by Antoine de Logiriera of Toulouse, a cow appears on the 2 of cups, although this detail does not seem to reappear until the late eighteenth century. Similarly an eagle appeared on the Logiriera ace of money as it does on the modern ace, but this detail has remained constant through the centuries. The modern 2 of clubs shows a little naked boy swinging on a rope slung between the two upright clubs. The female cavaliers, of course, are undoubtedly the most unusual feature of this pack. The axe-wielding king of money and the hand-on-hip halberdier jack of cups are two of the more obviously traditional figures and have always been features of *aluette* cards. Two other cards which distinguished the pack and remained constant both before and after 1776 are the 4 and 5 of money. The former has at its centre a six-pointed star and on the centre coin of the 5 the heads of a man and woman facing—nowadays usually kissing—one another.

The 5 of money, however (called rather unfairly *L'indécent*), provides some sort of key to the origins of the pack, for, in very early versions, this two-headed portrait is almost identical in form with the design of a coin of 1480 depicting Ferdinand

ROI D'EPEE.

XVIII

LA LUNE

CAVALIER DE DENIER.

Fig. 24. Italian-suited tarot cards as used in France and Switzerland: compare with fig. 4.

and Isabella of Spain. The earliest version of the card I have
so far seen is dated 1587 but the close likeness is unmistakable.
The ace of money prior to 1776 (and for a few years after this in
parts of France other than Brittany) often provided some clue to
dating, for it often carried Spanish arms and a legend mention-
ing the monarch of the time: an extra point to note is that after
1700, when the Spanish Bourbons came to the throne, a small
shield or inescutcheon bearing three fleurs-de-lis is found
at the centre of the arms.

See fig. 23 and plate I.

The Tarot de Marseille

This Italian-suited tarot pack has already been referred to
in the chapter dealing with Italian tarot cards, and there is very
little to add. The composition and the customary French
inscriptions on these cards are given on pp. 32, 33. The variations of 'Juno' and 'Jupiter' on trumps number II and V
emanated from Besançon around 1800, but such cards were also
known in Switzerland, so one should seek other means of
positive identification. An eighteenth-century pack from
Strasbourg had LE PRINTEMPS on trump number II and
another pack from Strasbourg substituted LA GRANDE MÈRE
and LE GRAND PÈRE for the two imperial trumps as well as
renaming the court cards *Egalité*, *Liberté* and *Génie* in honour
of the Revolution. The courts and trumps are always shown
single-figured and, apart from a few eighteenth-century cards
made in northern Italy by French cardmakers, are always rather
larger than their Italian cousins. Apart from inscriptions giving
maker and place-name, however, they are not so easy to
distinguish from early German and Swiss tarot cards.

See fig. 24.

French-suited tarots

These have never been as popular in France as they have
elsewhere, although they are still in use in eastern parts of the
country today. The present pattern, which seems to have been
in use for nearly a century, probably has its origins in Austria

Fig. 25. A trump card, the joker and the knight of hearts (suit-mark omitted) from a standard French-suited tarot pack as used in France and Switzerland. Similar cards were also issued in Germany and Austria.

and shows on the trumps a series of double-ended domestic and rural scenes. There is often a scrolled design at each end of the trump cards and the numbers are in Arabic figures. The pack comprises seventy-eight cards with the usual four suits of 14 cards and 22 trumps. In spite of their limited appeal, at least three companies in France were producing them in 1960.

See fig. 25.

Pl. III. Examples of differing styles. *Top row from left:* Lenthall's 'Love Motto' cards of circa 1710; J. Gole's Dutch 'Masquerade' cards (1691); 'All the Bubbles' of about 1720. *Centre left:* Italian version of geographical pack of about 1680 (see page 137); *right:* from 'Marlborough's Victories' (a new view of Mme de Maintenon), circa 1710. *Lower row:* from 'The Pretended Popish Plot' of about 1678, and Morden's geographical card of about 1710; note Lenthall border.

RE DI SPADE

CAPIT. NO FRACASSE

LESPAGNOL

LA PAPESSA

Plate IV

CHAPTER IV

Germany

CARD PLAYING seems to have hit medieval Bavaria like a thunderbolt. The idea of playing cards must have crossed the Brenner Pass almost as soon as it reached northern Italy, and the German printers immediately set out to provide what were probably the first printed cards to be made, in response to great public enthusiasm towards the novelty. Efforts on the part of city authorities to eradicate the time-wasting craze met with little response, and production soared. German card production has been prodigious ever since; and the imaginative and artistic approach to card design, particularly from the eighteenth century onward, far outpaced that of her neighbours with the possible exception of Austria. Although, to begin with, most cards were made in the south in such cities as Augsburg, Munich, Nuremberg and Ulm, when the other regions of what is now Germany entered the card-making field they too contributed a great deal to maintaining the high quality of German cards. This, however, did not always apply to standard cards, which from the beginning have been of simple design. The weight of public demand often resulted in shoddy design and production.

A number of very early blocks or their products have survived and provide a charming and quaint glimpse of what must be some of the earliest examples of popular art. All these blocks produced cards with German suit-marks of hearts, acorns,

Plate IV. *Top right and left:* standard Italian tarot cards. *Top centre and bottom right:* eighteenth-century Belgian and nineteenth-century Swiss or south-eastern French versions of *atout* II. *Centre right:* a seventeenth-century *minchiate* 'knight' of cups. The three cards at lower left are characteristic trappola cards of the eighteenth and nineteenth centuries.

hawkbells and leaves. They appear to be packs of forty-eight cards with court cards of king (German kings are always seated), over-knave and under-knave (*König, Ober* and *Unter*), although in some packs the under-knave is shown as a woman: the difference between *Ober* and *Unter* can be judged by the position of the suit-mark on the card. The pip cards were 2–9 and an additional card, a banner, took the place of the 10. This curious card is no longer used in Germany but can be found in modern Swiss-suited packs. (See fig. 3.)

Several details have survived from the earliest days of German cardmaking, such as lions on some deuces of acorns or wild boars on the deuce of bells, but the regional patterns probably did not attain any degree of standardization until about the seventeenth century. The pattern most resembling the early cards is one used in a tiny area of Germany today, known as the Ansbach portrait. Other figures known on very early cards are also found on the Bavarian and Franconian packs which also have several figures in common.

The latter patterns are shared with neighbouring countries and are known in Austria as the Salzburger pattern and in Czechoslovakia as the Bohemian pattern respectively. Confusion is therefore quite possible, although most cards of this type carry the names of makers and towns of origin quite clearly.

These three packs are clearly the oldest of the German-suited packs. Next probably comes the Saxon pattern, then the Württemberg-Palatine pack which incorporates the distinguishing feature of a mounted *Ober*, closely followed by the Prussian pattern which does not appear to go back beyond the beginning of the nineteenth century.

The Prussian pattern is probably the one most widely used today and a version of it is still being made in Poland. German-suited cards were known in Russia for a time, including the Prussian pattern, and I have bought a pack as far west as the Rhine, which gives some idea of its sphere of use.

Nowadays, however, German-suited cards are in the minority all over Germany. If standard English bridge cards are not used, the Berliner or north German pattern is the most prevalent. This is a florid, double-ended version of the Paris pattern, and has been in use for over 150 years. It probably took over from the so-called Bavarian French pattern, which was a single-figure version of the Paris pattern in the eighteenth century, and which also was used, plus the extra court card, on French-suited tarot cards.

Italian-suited tarot cards were used in Germany until the advent of the French-suited ones in mid-eighteenth century. Their age makes them extremely rare but when found they are notable for the execrable spelling on the trumps and court cards, which are (supposedly) inscribed in French. The French-suited tarots (or *Cego* cards) seem to sway before outside influences. The use of these cards is now apparently limited to the old state of Baden.

Standard cards in Germany reflect the days when Germany was a mass of separate states. Just as the states have become engulfed in the whole, so the cards are slowly but surely doing the same. Two or three makers still produce the old-fashioned regional patterns but, as has happened already to packs in Austria and Italy, the day may soon come when first one and then another of the old patterns will be dropped completely. It is my advice to collectors to get these cards represented in their collection as soon as possible. In Austria few people can remember what trappola cards were like after hundreds of years of use—they seem to have been casualties of the Second World War—and already in Germany people tend to look blank at the mention of, say, the *Ansbachbild*.

The Bavarian pattern (*bayrische*)

German suits. Thirty-six cards. Four suits of 9 (deuce, king, over-knave, under-knave, 6–10). Known with single-figure and double-headed courts. King of bells usually (in single-figure cards) has hand resting on Bavarian shield. The leaf court cards and over-knave of bells are almost identical with those of the Franconian or Sudeten pack, otherwise the distinguishing cards are: Deuce of hearts; a blindfolded cupid is portrayed in an elaborate frame; this is often the card on which a duty stamp appears. Deuce of acorns; a little boy holding a glass or tankard sits on a barrel. Deuce of bells; a boarhound leaps upon his quarry. Under the suit-marks on the pip cards various little vignettes show a series of simple leisure pastimes.

The Austrian Salzburger pattern which is otherwise almost indistinguishable from the Bavarian, does not carry the Bavarian coat-of-arms on the king of bells' shield.

See figs. 26A and 26B.

The Franconian or Sudeten pattern (Sudeten-deutsch)

German suits. Thirty-two cards. Four suits of 8 (deuce, king,

Fig. 26A. The Bavarian pattern: these two cards show single-figure courts. Note the position of the suit-marks on the *Ober* and *Unter* cards.

over-knave and under-knave, 7–10). Known with single-figure and double-headed court cards. Unlike the Bavarian cards, the

knaves of this pack are clearly divided into four military
categories. Those of hearts carry long spears or halberds; those
of acorns carry a sword in each hand; those of bells bear a single
sword; and the knaves of leaves play musical instruments.
Unlike Bavarian kings, Franconian kings have two suit-marks
on their cards.

See fig. 33, under Bohemian pattern in next chapter.

The Ansbach or Nuremberg pattern (Ansbach or Nürnberger Bild)
German suits. Thirty-six cards. Four suits of 9 (deuce, king,
over-knave, under-knave, and 6–10). Single-figure courts only.

 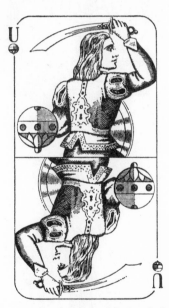

Fig. 26B. The Bavarian pattern. These cards show double-headed
courts.

These cards are distinctively simple in design, and the pip cards
carry no decorative vignettes. The deuces of hearts and bells,
for instance, carry no detailed decoration beyond, sometimes,
a surrounding wreath. Apart from the over-knave of acorns,
the knaves are all non-military in appearance and wear medieval

Fig. 27. The Ansbach or
Nuremberg pattern. Compare
the same cards in the Saxon
pack (fig. 28), the Württemberg pack (fig. 29) and the
Prussian pack (fig. 30).

Fig. 28. The Saxon pattern, with single-figure courts.

clothes with wide skirts. The knaves of leaves distinguish themselves by holding on to their suit-marks which have long stems. See fig. 27.

The Saxon pattern (sächsisch-thüringische)

German suits. Thirty-two or thirty-six cards. Four suits of 8 or 9 (deuce, king, over-knave, under-knave, 7–10 or 6–10). Known with single-figure and double-headed courts. The clothing on the knaves seemed to change with the years although their position and activity has remained the same. This pack is usually described on the deuce of acorns as being *Schwerdter* or *Schwerter Karte*, presumably referring to the swords which appear on the deuce of hearts. This description often has some adjective preceding it, such as *superfeine*, *feine extrafeine* or *neue*. The Saxon coat-of-arms is shown on both the deuce of acorns (under a lion's head) and the deuce of leaves. The deuce of bells shows a loving couple about to be discovered by a third person. The under-knave of bells has a bird perched on his wrist. Two suit-marks appear on the king cards of each suit. The vignettes at the foot of the pip cards are not constant, but are often rather grotesque and violent. I have, for instance, an 8 of leaves on which a monkey is sawing off the tail of a dog. See fig. 28.

The Württemberg-Palatine pattern (württembergische)

German suits. Thirty-six cards or, for the game of *Gaigel*, 2 x 24 cards. In the 36-card pack the cards of each suit comprise the usual deuce, king, over-knave (who is mounted), under-knave, and 6–10: in the 24-card version, the cards are deuce, king, mounted over-knave, under-knave, 7 and 10. This pack probably evolved from a cut-down version of tarot cards, which accounts for the mounted knaves and also for the fact that similar figures appear on fuller French-suited tarot packs in nineteenth and twentieth century Bavaria. The courts and pip cards are both double-ended, and I have never come across a single-ended version. Bottles of wine and grapes appear on the deuce of hearts, a steaming punch-bowl and ladle on

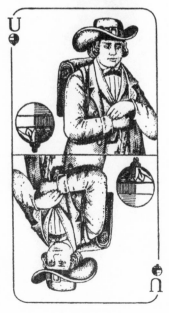

Fig. 29. The Württemberg
pattern: note the mounted
Ober.

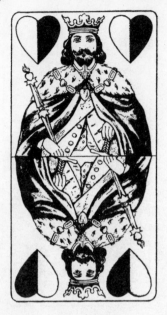

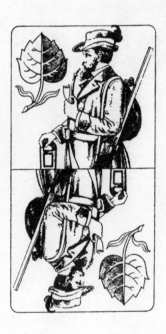

Fig. 30. The Prussian pattern with double-headed courts.

acorns, a goblet on bells and more wine bottles on leaves. The under-knave of bells has a satchel on his back. Although the clothing of the over-knaves varies in age and style, that of the under-knaves is limited to rural styles of the early nineteenth century. See fig. 29.

The Prussian pattern (*preussische*)

German suits. Thirty-two cards. Four suits of 8 cards (deuce, king, over-knave, under-knave, and 7–10). Known with single-figure and double-headed court cards. Kings have two suit-marks (four on double-headed version). Nowadays pip cards show famous buildings and towns, but older examples of the pack show more variety of design. The under-knaves make this pack particularly easy to identify:—

Hearts; a well-dressed nineteenth-century young man holds a bottle in his right hand, sometimes dated. Bells; a student holds a slate with a figure written on it. Leaves; a young hunter holds up a dead bird. A huntress with bow and arrows is shown on the deuce of leaves and (a figure reminiscent of the Bavarian pack but garlanded with vine leaves) a boy with a goblet sitting on a barrel. The deuce of hearts displays a fully-armed Brunnhilde-type of maiden. See fig. 30.

North-west Germany or Berliner pattern

French suits. Nowadays usually thirty-two or thirty-six cards but also known as a 52-card pack. Although basically a version of the Paris pattern, the jacks have all been reclothed in medieval German attire. Only known with double-headed courts, but, as I have already pointed out, the single-figure Bavarian pack of the eighteenth century was probably its direct ancestor. It is hard to give any hard-and-fast rule with regard to placing this pack as definitely German in origin, as other countries—particularly the Scandinavian—adopted very similar designs. Nevertheless, a maker's name and town are usually to be found somewhere on the cards. See fig. 31.

The French-suited Bavarian pattern

French suits. Fifty-two or fifty-six(?) cards. In the British

Fig. 31. The N.W. German
version of the Paris pattern;
the jack of hearts is shown
with suit-mark omitted.

Museum there are some examples of 56-card packs of this pattern which are identical in composition and design to the suit section of a tarot pack. The many versions of tarot games in southern Germany may well account for the absence of the trump cards and the presence of the knight but I am not yet wholly convinced that these packs were not in fact simply tarot packs which lacked the trumps. In my own collection I have such a pack made by A. B. Göbl of Munich but I also have a full tarot pack by the same maker with cards obviously made from the same plates.

To return to the design of these cards; they were undoubtedly the most attractive variation of the Paris pattern ever to evolve. The cards were much larger and longer than the French ones and a great deal of intricate detail was incorporated in the clothing and accoutrements of the court cards. It is very sad that such fine examples of the cardmaker's art should have given way to the mundane and often severe design of the later Berliner cards.

French-suited tarot cards (nowadays Cego cards)

French suits. Seventy-eight or fifty-four cards. The 78-card pack comprised four suits of fourteen cards (ace, king, queen, knight, jack and 2–10) plus twenty-two trump cards: the 54-card pack comprised four suits of eight cards (hearts and diamonds; king, queen, knight, jack and ace–4: spades and clubs; king, queen, knight, jack and 7–10) plus twenty-two trump cards. The 78-card pack was used widely throughout Bavaria during the second half of the eighteenth century and the beginning of the nineteenth, but its popularity declined and the 54-card pack used in Baden is all that now remains. The design of standard packs of these cards tends to overlap, so it is only possible to lay down a few generalities for the collector.

The first standard design for the suit cards was undoubtedly the same as the 52-card Bavarian pack (see above), and this was to remain constant for about sixty years (between c. 1760 and 1820). It also spread to the then Austrian-ruled Belgium where the first-known series of trump cards remained constant until the early twentieth century—far longer than in the area of its probable origin. This pattern is sometimes called 'animal tarots' and the trump cards thereof show a constant series of animals (with a few inevitable exceptions from time to time) although the order in which they appear seems to differ from maker to maker. A performing bear, however, usually turns up on trump XXI and other animals include a unicorn, camel, turkey, deer, lion and boar. The trumps and courts are always single-figure, and the numbers on the trumps in roman figures.

Fashion soon proved stronger than tradition; in Germany, that is. Cardmakers, while retaining the standard court cards design, vied with one another to produce the most attractive or unusual series of trump cards (some are described in the chapter on non-standard cards). The nearest to a standard pattern that emerged at the beginning of the nineteenth century still made use of natural history subjects with double-ended trump cards and courts, although the solitary figures of the old animal tarots had disappeared.

Thereafter the taste for *Cego* and the 54-card pack seems to have coincided with the appearance of a new set of standard court cards (double-headed and nineteenth-century in flavour); the trumps in such packs vary in their subject matter but often show scenes from nineteenth-century life and bear Arabic numerals. These are similar in many respects to the modern French and Swiss packs.

Italian-suited tarot cards

As previously mentioned, these cards disappeared from Germany at the time when the French-suited tarots became popular. They appeared principally in the south-west, and until about 1750 they had the same composition as the French *tarot de Marseille* but with extremely poor, obviously phonetic, spelling on the court cards and trumps. In the mid-eighteenth century there is some evidence that packs were made with Italian suit-marks but the later type of trump cards had animal subjects. Whether this was a stage of transition or whether people merely made up imperfect packs with whatever material they could lay their hands on, I do not know.

Trappola cards

These cards are more fully described under Austria where they were more widely used: however, German-made packs occasionally turn up, although they have never been much in use there. Briefly, they have Italian suit-marks, and there are thirty-six cards to the pack—ace, king, knight, jack, 2 and 7–10.

CHAPTER V

The Austro-Hungarian Empire

PART of the enjoyment of a collecting hobby is that one can indulge in one's own particular favourites. The serious collector will call it specialization, but in his heart of hearts he really knows that he has succumbed to a completely shameless piece of favouritism. This is how I feel about the cards of Austria.

In the first place the cards from the area which was formerly the Austro-Hungarian Empire are immensely varied. The passion for all kinds of card-playing which struck Italy and Germany in the fifteenth century and France a little later led to a heyday in quantity and quality of card production in the eighteenth century: however, in the Empire, which absorbed the idea of cards at the same time, an enthusiasm for elegance of design and quality seems to have reached its climax in the nineteenth century—with the result that more fine cards have survived than from almost any other part of Europe.

Today, particularly in Austria but to some degree also in those parts of the old Empire which have come under Communist control, a high standard of card production is maintained and with few exceptions the traditional patterns remain in use. If you should visit Dubrovnik in Yugoslavia, you will still find cards with German or Italian suits of patterns which have their origin in the Empire. In Budapest, the standard German-suited pack with the four seasons shown on the deuces can still be bought, just as it can be found in Vienna; I have not traced a post-World War II example of the pack made in Prague.

Another reason why I like these cards is that they display such wide differences in the style of art applied to them, often according to the district or the individual cardmaker. The colours are gay, the subject matter is usually lively, and treatment, particularly of the French-suited tarot cards of the nineteenth century, is often highly imaginative.

The standard packs of the Empire are easily distinguished one from another. They all appear to have been in general use but one or two have special regional affiliations and are named accordingly. To me they are representative of almost every stage in the evolution of playing cards and their design evokes numerous aspects of the many peoples who made up the Empire and who still cling to at least one small part of it in their cards.

It has been said that *trappola* cards are as old or older than the Italian tarot pack. I have never been able to trace any proof of this, so can only pass on the tradition for what it is worth. Clearly, however, this Italian-suited pack is a very old one, and examples thought to belong to the sixteenth century are known. But its very composition with cards omitted from the usual 1–10 sequence of pip cards implies that it evolved from some earlier pack, probably the north-eastern Italian packs referred to in a previous chapter. Certainly the name of this pack is Italian, the word meaning literally 'a trick', although the word has been corrupted in some German-speaking provinces and has variations such as *Trappolier*, *Trappulier* or even, in Poland, *Traplaczka*. In Czechoslovakia they are known as *Spady* cards.

Unhappily the game and the pack have, after centuries, disappeared from the card-playing scene. As far as I can make out, the last packs were probably made in Prague just before World War II. It took me six years to track down my first example of this type of card with its exotic kings, dashing knights and colourful jacks, but, such is the joyous uncertainty of collecting, I then proceeded to acquire eight more, of varying age and origins, all from quite different sources.

Generally speaking they were used throughout the Empire, but they were made principally in Prague, Graz and Vienna.

Technically speaking, the Venetian, Trentine and Triestine cards might also be said to be Italian-suited cards from within the limits of the Empire, but as they now seem so much part of modern Italy, I have already described them under that heading. However, the Triestine is still obtainable, as I have said, in Yugoslavia. Italian-suited tarots were also known in the Empire before the development of the preferred French-suited tarot in the eighteenth century. Examples of these are extremely rare and my remarks concerning similar cards in Germany apply here also (see page 94).

There are three different German-suited packs in the Imperial territory. Two have links with Germany, and have been mentioned already—the Salzburger and Bohemian patterns—and the third, which was in use throughout the provinces of the Empire, has a unique characteristic in standard cards, that of having *mounted* kings. This pack is sometimes called Hungarian, but it was obviously used also in Austria, Bohemia, and Bosnia and I have therefore dubbed it The Seasons pattern, from the scenes shown on the deuces. The over-knaves and under-knaves of this pack are usually named and portray medieval Central European heroes. Although I cannot trace any really early examples of these cards, they share some characteristics to be found on cards dated 1583 which are now in the British Museum.

The French-suit pattern, which was the most widely used, must have evolved from an old seventeenth-century design first found in Lyons. Its subsequent history is very sketchy, but from odd packs that have turned up it seems likely that at first they were exported from Lyons to regions which are now French-Switzerland, and from there to Lombardy and Venetia and ultimately the design was copied and came into common use throughout Austria and Bohemia. This may well be an example of how the fashion for a certain game will spread a special type of card. The present-day example of this is bridge and poker, for which English-style cards are everywhere preferred. It looks as though the game which introduced the French-styled cards into the Empire may well have been piquet, as the packs are usually made up of thirty-two cards. Nowadays many other games are played with them, and in Bohemia at least the full 52-card pack is employed.

There are, in fact, two versions of the pack still made in the

Empire area. The main version (which I will call Pattern A for convenience) is used throughout Austria and also in Czechoslovakia, and the subsidiary (Pattern B) is, so far as I know, only found in Czechoslovakia. The difference is one of style rather than detail, but it is quite pronounced.

Apart from these patterns, standard French-suited cards from other countries turn up from time to time, but these were probably produced at the whim of fashion and cannot really be said to belong to the Empire. Presumably such events as an alliance with Prussia, or a marriage with France, would account for such phenomena.

Finally, the glory of Imperial cardmaking—the French-suited tarot. There is in fact more cause for rhapsodizing in the section on non-standard cards, as it is in the huge variety of subjects and themes which appear on the trump cards, which range from the artistic to the ingenious and comic in their content, that makes these tarots such a unique commentary on nineteenth-century social and political history. However, the standard pattern which emerged at some time during the middle of the last century is of great interest on its own account and is a fine example of the quality to be expected in the production of these cards. The pack is still used for a number of games in Austria, and may be so behind the Iron Curtain too, for it was being produced in Czechoslovakia until at least 1939.

Trappola cards

Italian suits. Thirty-six cards. Four suits comprising ace, king, knight, jack, 2 and 7–10. Known with single-figure courts and also double-headed courts and aces. They are easily distinguished from Italian packs by the form of the pack and the Roman-figure indices on the pip cards, as well as the following characteristics on individual cards: The courts of the cups and swords suits have a decidedly oriental influence in their dress, whereas the courts of the money and club suits depict western or at least imperial figures. The ace of cups shows an eagle perched on the top. The maker's name appears on the ace of clubs.

These cards vary tremendously in size, some being as much
as six inches high. They are usually narrow but come in all
shapes and sizes; they are usually brightly coloured and
extremely attractive. Unfortunately they are not in current use.
I have found in the past that such is the mystique of these cards
that any unidentified pack of thirty-six cards is described by
dealers or other sellers as a trappola pack: naturally one can
make up any type of pack into the required number for any
game, but true trappola cards are described above and anything
else offered as such should be evaluated accordingly.

See plate IV.

Salzburg pattern (Salzburger)

German suits. Thirty-six or thirty-two cards. Four suits of
8 or 9 cards, comprising deuce, king, over-knave, under-knave
and 6 or 7–10. This pattern has substantially been described
under the Bavarian pattern on page 83. One difference often
apparent in modern versions of the cards is the introduction of
the inscription WELI on the 6 of bells, together with one pip
each of the suits of acorns and hearts. This characteristic is also
known in the Seasons pattern, but I do not know of it ever
occurring outside Austria. Salzburger cards always have single-
figure courts. (See fig. 32.)

Bohemian pattern (Böhmisch Deutsche)

German suits. Thirty-two cards. Four suits of 8 cards (deuce,
king, over-knave and under-knave, and 7–10). This pattern has
already been described under the Franconian pattern on page
84. The Bohemian version, however, has a far wider use. The
maker's name is usually found on the deuce of acorns where an
enigmatic-looking animal, probably a lion, appears underneath.
The two-tailed Czech lion is in evidence on the deuce of hearts,
but it depends on the age of the cards as to whose coats-of-arms
appear on the deuce of bells. The vignettes at the foot of the
pip cards seem to remain fairly constant, a particularly noticeable one being the dying bird transfixed by the stem of the 9 of

acorns. With very occasional exceptions, these cards are single-figured.

See fig. 33.

The Seasons pattern

German suits. Twenty-four, thirty-two or thirty-six cards.

Fig. 32. The 'WELI' card which is found in many German-suited Austrian packs and a pip card showing a typical style of vignette for most German-suited packs.

Four suits of 6 or 8 or 9 cards (deuce, mounted king, over-knave, under-knave and 6– or 7– or 9–10). The deuces on which the Seasons are portrayed are usually inscribed in German, sometimes in Hungarian, occasionally in English and once in a while not at all. They are as follows, with the German and Hungarian words in parentheses:

Deuce of hearts: Spring (*Frühling* or *Tavasz*)

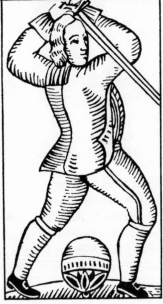

Fig. 33. The Bohemian
pattern, sometimes called the
Prager pattern. This is almost
identical with the Franconian
pack.

Deuce of acorns: Winter (*Winter* or *Tél*)
Deuce of bells: Summer (*Sommer* or *Nyar*)
Deuce of leaves: Autumn (*Herbst* or *Osz*)

It should be noted that some of these cards made in Hungary have German inscriptions.

All the cards are double-ended and I have not so far found a recognizable version with single figures although the kings have appeared in certain Austro-Hungarian packs from the sixteenth century. The knave cards are usually named and it is a quirk of the Hungarian language that the surname is given first. *Wilhelm Tell* on the over-knave of acorns becomes, therefore, *Tell Vilmos*. *Walter Fürst* on the under-knave of leaves becomes *Fürst Walter*. So far, the versions of the pack which I have found emanating from Prague have either had no inscriptions at all or merely English ones on the deuces: nevertheless there seems to be no reason why such cards should not have existed with Czech inscriptions.

See fig. 34.

French-suited Pattern A

Thirty-two cards. Four suits comprising ace, king, queen, jack and 7–10. The maker's name usually appears on the king of spades' sash, and the name of the city of origin on a banner held by the jack of hearts. All the kings wear high crowns with a top made flat by the design's frameline. The king of hearts carries a scroll in his hand (originally this was thought to be a fan) which is sometimes found inscribed with a misleading date, probably the date of origin of the design for the set of plates being used. Cards are still being produced by Piatnik of Vienna, having the date 1885 on this scroll. The queen of clubs, who was originally the square-ermine-sleeved lady of early French cards, still wears heavily ermined but rounded sleeves. The jack of clubs carries a corrupt version of an ancient weapon which now looks more like a carpet-beater than anything else.

I have not found many old versions of this pack which is only a ghost of its old French ancestors, and none with single-figured courts, save a nineteenth-century Swiss pack which is

Fig. 34. The Seasons pattern which here have German inscriptions. On the right is the deuce of leaves, representing Autumn.

clearly related. When the pattern first came to the Empire is not known but by the middle of the last century it was very firmly established. See also under Lyonnais pattern, on page 69.

See fig. 35.

French-suited Pattern B

Fifty-two cards. It has many characteristics in common with Pattern A; the banner-holding jack of hearts, the deep-brimmed hat of the jack of diamonds, the flat-topped headdresses of the queens of hearts and spades and the maker's name on the sash worn by the king of spades, for instance. The identifying differences which are the easiest to spot are as follows: the kings' crowns are shown in full, with irregular tops which do not touch the frame line; the king of hearts holds a sceptre and not a scroll; the queen of clubs carries a hand mirror. This pattern, too, I have so far found only with double-headed court cards.

Both packs usually contain aces of spades and hearts which give a bonus in descriptive information—maker's name and address and tax stamp.

Tarot cards (Tarock)

French suits. Fifty-four or seventy-eight cards. Four suits of 8 or 14 (king, queen, knight, jack, and hearts and diamonds ace–4, and spades and clubs 7–10 for the 54-card pack; and king, queen, knight, jack and ace–10 for the 78-card pack) plus twenty-two trump cards. Generally speaking the trump cards depict scenes of outdoor life in various countries. Details of these scenes vary, but the theme remains constant: Turks and Arabs continue to mingle with Scotsmen and Danes. The trumps and court cards are double-ended and the trumps show a different scene at each end. They are numbered with Roman figures. Trump number II used invariably to have at one end the picture of a crowned eagle, sword in claw, perched on a rock inscribed with INDUSTRIE UND GLUCK. Republican Czechoslovakia, however, took the eagle's crown away and altered the inscription to AUDACES FORTUNA JUVAT. Two itinerant musi-

Fig. 35. A nineteenth-century
version of the Austrian
French-suited pack.

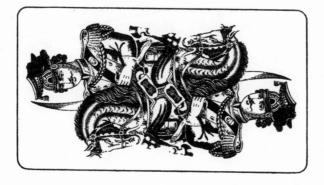

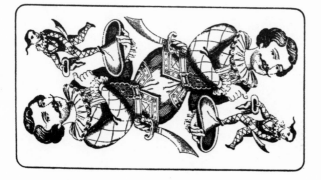

Fig. 36. The standard Austrian French-suited tarot pattern as used in the last century. The suit-mark is omitted from the knight of diamonds.

cians (one male, one female) are depicted on trump number I. The maker's name and address are given on the jacks of diamonds and clubs and maker's stamp and tax stamp appear on the ace of hearts. The figures on the court cards are elaborately clothed.

This pattern has certainly been in use for over a hundred years and has provided many examples of fine art work and beautiful printing.

See fig. 36.

CHAPTER VI

Switzerland and the Rest

WHEN cards began their lengthy history, Switzerland as such did not exist—the eight cantons of the ancient Swiss Confederation cannot have taken up more than about a quarter of the territory covered by present-day Switzerland. Yet, from that tiny area, with its strongly Germanic influences, a national suit-system evolved which is still in use today and which has an interest at least as great as many of its more widely used neighbours. These cards, with their suit-marks of shields, acorns, hawkbells and flowers were established by the early sixteenth century although it seems likely that their origins could safely be put a hundred years earlier. Even today these cards have a distinguishing feature, not found elsewhere after the sixteenth century, in their display of a banner with a single suit-mark (or double in the instance of double-ended cards) in place of the usual 10 of any suit. The coats-of-arms or devices shown on the shields suit have remained fairly constant but whether they represent an early lesson in heraldry, or the nobility of the time, I have not been able to discover: at any rate they do not appear to have any connection with the arms of the cantons themselves.

As new cantons joined the Confederation they brought with them the customs of other lands. Italian-suited tarot cards were early imports and are still made and used. French-suited cards in the Paris pattern appeared from the direction of France and when many Lyonnais cardmakers were driven by heavy taxes into Switzerland at the end of the sixteenth century it seems probable that they brought their local cards with them too (see page 69). When fashion decreed French-suited tarot packs Switzerland followed along. Finally, when the Ticino joined the Confederation, the French-suited Milanese pack (see page 52) joined with it.

Today, there are five standard packs used in Switzerland—plus an extra, offshoot Italian-suited tarot pack which seems to be popular and long-lived enough to be regarded as standard.

These packs are recognizable as follows:

Fig. 37A. The distinctive Swiss-suit pattern showing single figure and double-headed cards.

Swiss-suit pack (Jasskarten)

Swiss suits of shields, acorns, hawk-bells and flowers. Nowadays thirty-six cards, although in the past 48-card packs, made in the district of Soleure, were known. The suits are made up of king, over-knave (*Ober*), under-knave (*Under*), 6–9, banner and deuce. The banner which originated as a 10 is now more or less counted as an ace, or at any rate as an extra court card. The suit-marks and the presence of the banners render it impossible to confuse the pattern with any other, but it has a

few other unique characteristics as well. The king of shields
sits with a canopy over his head and a goblet of wine in hand.
The under-knave of shields carries a letter and has a quill pen
either behind his ear or clenched between his teeth. The over-
knaves of acorns and bells are smoking pipes and the head of
the under-knave of bells is as round as the sun and has a

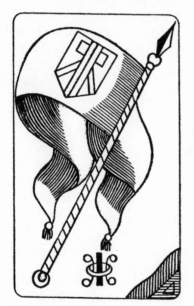 

Fig. 37B. A single-figure banner or 10 of shields and a deuce of
flowers.

flamelike head dress. All court cards are named with their
rank. The maker's name is usually found on the deuce of shields
and his place of origin on the deuce of bells. The cards are
known with single-figure and double-ended court cards.

See Figs. 37A. and 37B.

Italian-suited tarot cards (tarot or taroc)

These are virtually indistinguishable from French or later
Italian single-figure tarot cards. Everything that has been said

about the *tarot de Marseille* can equally be said about these cards: the maker's name and address is the only hope of positive identification. It always has single-figure trump cards and courts. (See fig. 24).

The offshoot pack mentioned above has a nineteenth-century flavour in its designs, but its chief distinguishing mark is that it is the only modern pack made with Juno and Jupiter on the trumps number II and V. I do not know if this is a nonconformist protest against the Papacy which was shared with the earlier Besançon tarot cards (see page 78), but it is a pack well worth having for its historical implications. It is now, like the majority of Swiss cards, made by J. Müller & Cie. of Schaffhausen.

French-Swiss pattern (used everywhere except Ticino)

Usually thirty-six cards (king, queen, jack, ace and 6–10). This version of the Paris pattern is very hard to distinguish from those of other countries (notably Sweden and Germany) unless a maker's name is in evidence. The court cards are known with single figures and double-ended, the latter having the central break as a horizontal rule.

Ticinese pattern (*ticinese*)

French suits. Forty cards. Four suits comprising king, queen, jack and ace–7. These cards are identical with the Milanese pattern (see fig. 16).

French-suited tarot (*taroc or tarot*)

Seventy-eight cards. Four suits of 14 (king, queen, knight, jack and ace–10,) and twenty-two numbered trump cards. These are almost identical with the French version of the pack (see fig. 25) and show domestic scenes on the trump cards. Court cards and trumps are double-headed. The trumps are numbered with Arabic figures.

The rest of Europe cannot claim much strong original continuity in its card design. Belgium (or rather the Low Countries) torn between a series of invaders employed cards introduced by them. Italian-suited tarots have survived from the eighteenth century with some intriguing characteristics which make them unique. Trump number II is titled *Capitano Eracasse—Lespagnol* and trump number V depicts Bacchus astride a barrel, but spelt *Bacus*. Trumps number XVII and XVIII and XXI provide one of the most fascinating riddles in the history of card design. Instead of following the conventional tarot designs, they employ the symbolism otherwise found only on Bolognese *tarocchino* cards and very early illuminated tarots.

	Traditional tarot design	*Tarocchino and Belgian*
XVII The Star	Under the Star a figure probably meant as *Aquarius* is emptying two jars of water.	Under the Star sits or stands a Navigator holding a pair of compasses.
XVIII The Moon	Two dogs bark at the Moon and a *Scorpio*-like creature emerges from water.	A spinner sits holding a distaff.
XXI The World	A wreath or garland surrounds a naked, youthful figure and the symbols for the Gospel Apostles appear one in each corner.	The naked figure, ungarlanded, stands on a huge orb on which is depicted sun, moon and earth.

The Tower or *Maison de Dieu* has been replaced in this pack by *La Foudre* and shows a tree being struck by lightning. An aid to play occurs on the 2 of cups belonging to a pack in my possession: '*pour conoistre que la plus basse de deniez et de coupes enporte les plus hautes quand au fait du ieu*'. All courts and trumps are inscribed in French and the spelling is arbitrary: the final crudity is perpetrated on trump number XII where the hanging man is shown the wrong way up and appears to be standing on tip toe. This card must be the one which has perpetuated a legend that the Hanging Man was originally a standing figure. Upon such misty evidence is much card lore based.

The French-suited pack used in Belgium is identical with the Genoese (see page 54) and is difficult to identify. During the last century and a half both Belgian and Dutch cardmakers have been shy of placing their names on their cards (with occasional exceptions) so that it is frequently impossible to identify the cards of these countries. The Dutch make it easier these days by having a semblance of a national French-suited pack based on the Paris pattern but distinctively drawn and having the indices H, V, B and A or 1 on the kings, queens, jacks and aces. The aces are frequently what are termed 'scenic aces'; they depict views of Dutch towns or countryside.

The Italian-suited tarot cards were replaced in Belgium by French-suited ones with animals portrayed on the trump cards. There appear always to have been seventy-eight cards in the pack used in this area: the type of pack has already been described in the German section on page 93.

Sweden and Russia both have their version of the Paris pattern, although the former seems now to have deserted tradition for cards which might be described as 'pretty'. Both countries in the past also used German-suited cards—both no longer do so. Examples of such cards are extremely rare. Although many Swedish cards have characteristics in common with their Scandinavian neighbours, the ace of hearts usually offers some clue to identity in the form of maker's or tax stamps. The jack of clubs sometimes provides a maker's name. The indices K, D, Kn, and E or Es are not infallible clues, but they at least narrow the field to Scandinavia. Pre-Revolutionary Russian cards are easily known by their tax stamp which depicts the sign of the Imperial Foundling Hospital (which was supported by the tax on cards) on the ace of diamonds: this is a pelican with outstretched wings tending her young. After the Revolution this source of income was redirected and the pelican disappeared. At first the royalty on the standard cards disappeared also, but finally the authorities relented, for today the old Paris pattern has returned. The indices on Russian cards have for the past sixty years or so been a firm giveaway, being K, Д, B and T.

Norway and particularly Denmark have for some time produced artistic and non-standard cards of a high quality. However, generally speaking they have turned to other countries for design.

Poland also seems to have adopted a number of designs, apparently desultorily, from other countries, particularly Germany and the Austro-Hungarian Empire. These include Trappola cards, Prussian pattern German-suited cards and several designs known in other parts of Europe although not quite in the category of standard so far as design goes. Indices on these Polish cards with French suits are K, D, W, and A.

I have to confess that I have not been able to dig further behind the Iron Curtain: Rumania and Bulgaria remain at present a closed book although I understand that the indices on Bulgarian cards are K, M, B and T. The division of the famous German company A.S.S. which fell into Communist hands exports to many countries.

Moving back across the Curtain, the final port of call is Greece which, so far as card playing is concerned, is a latecomer. Presumably the Turkish domination at a crucial time delayed the introduction of the habit. Initially cards with French, Italian or English influence found favour, doubtless reflecting various occupations and subsequent liberations (most cards being made in the island of Corfu), but in the twentieth century there emerged a pattern which appears to have settled down into common usage, although even today card playing is not as popular in Greece as it is elsewhere. The court cards portray ancient heroes of Greece, and the indices on courts and aces are B, K, Θ, and Α.

It is hoped that a framework has been provided for a fuller picture of card playing and its history. In order to provide aids to identification a good deal of detailed description has been necessary. I myself have found, however, that this background information is invaluable in appreciating the full richness of card design and its historical significance. Most non-standard cards are superior in design to the standard packs but because serious card-players are conservative about the cards they use, most packs with unusual designs are produced with some additional purpose in mind—education, propaganda, or diversion. In the following section I shall attempt to fill in the rest of the history of cards. It would be quite impossible to give a complete listing or description of non-standard cards even if any one person had accumulated the relevant information, for the production of such cards has always been, and still is, quite overwhelming. However, definite trends can be discerned from early times, and some account of these may help collectors to bring the history of cards (including their own) into some sort of perspective.

PART II

The Non-Standard Cards of Europe

CHAPTER VII

Trends prior to 1800

STANDARD cards are used for card games. Non-standard cards are seldom put to such use, but it depends greatly on the age and circumstances in which they are produced as to what purpose they fulfil. Early German engravers saw packs of cards as fifty-two (or more, or less) frames for intricate artistic themes. Cardinal Mazarin is said to have considered a pack of cards as a means to catch the wandering attention of a young king, and so four packs, all beautifully engraved by the Florentine Stefano Della Bella, were issued by Desmarests, carrying educational messages (see page 127). The anti-Roman Catholic pamphleteers of seventeenth-century England saw packs of cards as compact series of fifty-two prints and captions—almost a sort of propaganda horror-comic. Anyone, in fact, who wished to produce a series of prints, whether on musical themes, a collection of proverbs, lessons in Latin grammar or heraldry, or, perhaps best suited of all, a description of the fifty-two counties of England and Wales, discovered that sales were helped by the added novelty of their being presented as a pack of cards.

Today the tradition persists. The novelty pack will catch the eye, it will be purchased either as a present for someone else or out of personal curiosity; it will not be used for card games (patience is, perhaps, the exception to this rule) and will probably remain in some drawer or cupboard until finally it is thrown away, sent to a jumble sale, or discovered by a collector. It is difficult to say whether standard or non-standard cards are the harder to find. In any event, the collector's life is a hard one. Searching for a pack of cards illustrating the moral precepts of the early eighteenth century in England is as elusive a quest

as looking for a wig or hat of the same period. Fashion ultimately destroys itself and it takes chance as well as perseverance
for last year's pack of mottoes to survive until such time as they
become of real historic interest.

Whatever the difficulties confronting the collector, however,
when these non-standard packs do appear, they are often of
genuine interest to the student of social history. Although I
have mentioned three categories of non-standard cards—
instructive, propagandist and diverting—each of these has a
great number of sub-divisions. Instructive can cover historical,
geographical, heraldic, mathematical, scientific, domestic or
grammatical cards. Propaganda was intended with the publication of the anti-Catholic cards mentioned above, with patriotic
versions of current events, with satirical and allegorical
criticism of contemporary institutions, with publicity and
advertising cards. The purely diverting cards, however, are the
most fascinating of all, reflecting the artistry, wit, prudery,
bawdiness, elegance, ugliness and ingenuity of so many different
times and places.

The first trend in non-standard cardmaking occurred in
Germany and resulted in some of the most intricate and beautiful cards ever to be made. Dürer is not known to have designed
cards but many of his most gifted contemporaries, both in the
field of engraving and painting, appear to have done so. The
cards which have survived from this period (late fifteenth and
early sixteenth century) are, needless to say, mostly found in
museums. Virtually the only hope the collector has of becoming
familiar with a pack of early engraved German cards is to
acquire a set of forty-seven reproductions of such cards issued
by Ottley in London in 1828 under the title of *Facsimiles of
Scarce and Curious Prints:* these are reproductions of a pack
attributed to Martin Schongauer; the originals must have
been made in about 1500. I show one of them on plate II. The
suit-marks are almost Italian, being swords, cups, clubs and
pomegranates instead of money. Every possible type of figure,
from cherub to centaur, is found entwined round the suit-
marks on the pip cards. There are banners for 10s and the courts

are king, queen and mounted knave. The Ottley reproductions are themselves quite scarce, but they do turn up from time to time and are well worth having.

The use of non-German or, in fact, wholly original suits was quite a well-known characteristic of these early cards. Pomegranates were found on other packs, as well as those mentioned above, and other curiosities (although beautiful ones) included some beautifully painted cards from Stuttgart (c. 1440) using dogs, stags, ducks and falcons as suit-marks, and a pack of round cards from Cologne (1470) employing parrots, roses, hares, pinks and columbines to make up five suits of thirteen cards each. Early in the sixteenth century Virgil Solis of Nuremberg engraved a pack depicting lions, monkeys, peacocks and parrots as suits. Jost Ammon produced in 1588 a book of fanciful cards with suit-marks of printers' inking balls, wine-pots, drinking cups and books, with a verse underneath each one: this was entitled *The Book of Trades* and was reproduced in Munich in 1880. I have never come across a copy, though it should be obtainable.

All these cards were peculiar to Germany at a particular period. The next appearance of German non-standard cards in any quantity is in the seventeenth century and is clearly related to a similar fashion for these cards which swept first through France and then through the rest of Europe. They retained in many instances their own suit-marks, but the craze for instruction through this medium was shared with France, the Low Countries, Spain and, to a lesser degree, Italy. Some of the earliest known geographical cards came from Germany in 1640, but use French suits.

The four packs engraved by Della Bella and issued by Jean Desmarests in 1644 started a trend in educational cards which lasted for 150 years. These are the cards said to have been suggested by Cardinal Mazarin to encourage the flagging educational interests of a royal charge. They were entitled *Jeu des Fables*, *Jeu des Rois de France*, *Jeu des Reynes Renommées*, and *Jeu de Géographie*. They must have been an instant success, for they are known in several different forms (sheets, books and packs), were copied in Germany, the Low Countries and Italy, and were still being reprinted and sold more than fifty years after their first appearance. (For description, see page 127.)

The first heraldic cards were probably those made by Claude Oroncé Finé, M. de Brianville, in Lyons in 1658–9. Clearly a knowledge of heraldry was necessary in the seventeenth century, and cards such as these filled a need, for a version of Brianville's *Jeu de Blason* was still available in Spain in the 1730s. Each card showed the coat-of-arms of various European states, with a short description underneath. The design remained fairly constant (although descriptions varied according to the language of the country of publication) except for the king of clubs whereon the papal arms were shown. The changes on this card made it possible to judge, more or less, the date of any particular edition of this pack. I have so far traced fifteen different editions of the cards—five in France, four in Italy, three in Holland and one each in England, Germany and Spain. They were also issued in book form and P. Mortier of Amsterdam (who seems to have copied nearly all the finest French packs of his period) published an explanatory volume in French which ran to at least eight editions. Bulifon of Naples issued a similar volume in Italian. Other heraldic packs were issued as time went on, notably Almaury's in Lyons in 1692 (a highly decorative pack with suit-marks of fleurs-de-lis, eagles, roses and lions), Silvestre's in Paris, c. 1700 (and reissued after a few years by Daumont); Richard Blome's in England in 1675 (this gave a thorough and general grounding in the whole art of heraldry); a 1686 pack giving the arms of the English peers; one by Walter Scott, an Edinburgh engraver, depicting the arms of the Scottish peers, and a rare item (of which there were two editions) from Italy dealing with the subject of Venetian heraldry (1682 and 1707).

Apart from a remarkable exception in Elizabethan times, educational cards did not appear in England until ten or twenty years after the Restoration—playing cards of any kind had, of course, been very much frowned upon by the Puritans. But we then made up for lost time, and English cardmakers portrayed a wide variety of themes on their wares. The art of carving, Latin grammar, mathematics, natural history, astronomy, heraldry, cooking were among the subjects chosen. All these cards are extremely rare, and are mostly to be found in museums. In the British Museum there is an advertisement for the cards published and sold by a stationer, John Lenthall, at the beginning of the eighteenth century, who had made and sold cards since the decade after the Restoration, and some of the cards referred to on the list must have been first printed around that time. The advertisement provides such an invaluable check-list of these early instructive cards that I reproduce it later in the chapter and describe as many of the packs mentioned as I have been able to identify.

Lenthall's list contains, as well as instructive cards, the earliest of a new wave of cards intended for amusement. These were of a fairly high artistic quality although they were not issued primarily as artistic cards. Buffoon cards from Holland showed grotesque theatrical characters on each of the pip cards: on English cards proverbs, moral precepts were illustrated, love mottoes provided the captions for another pack. One category of card, however, Lenthall did not advertise, and that was the propaganda card unless it had a patriotic theme.

England seems to have been the first country to have employed cards as political criticism or commentary. The first of such packs may have been one lampooning the Commonwealth Government and the Rump Parliament, but the principal series of such packs directed its vituperation and imaginative slander against one target—the Catholic Church. There were a number of such packs but the most popular, and as a result perhaps the least rare, was clearly *The Popish Plot*, for which there was such demand that four different sets of plates had to be engraved and used in the course of its publication.

By the time Queen Anne came to the throne, the political pamphleteers had quietened down, and patriotism became enough. *The Events of the Reign of Queen Anne* and *Marlborough's Victories* show Queen Anne as the scourge of tyrants (and Marlborough the scourge of practically everyone else). Then in

about 1710 the friends of Dr Sacheverell were greatly concerned when this divine was impeached for preaching two
sermons thought by some to be politically unsound: in order
to arouse public opinion on the side of the doctor, a pack of
cards was issued in his defence.

This particular age of satire and commentary was rapidly
coming to an end: England seemed to prefer less uncomfortable
themes for her cards. The last cards to show serious criticism
appeared in two packs issued around 1720—*The South Sea
Bubble* and *All the Bubbles*. Both are fascinating, though unfortunately rare, and provide excellent examples of the humour
and biting wit of the time as well as highlighting the perpetual
stupidity of greedy man. The *All the Bubbles* deals with a
wonderful selection of 'projects' of the time: some of them
died, or perhaps burst with The Bubble, others, such as Life
Insurance and Populating the Bahamas had the seeds of good
ideas.

Another rare but famous pack of the same period is that
devoted to *The Beggar's Opera*, giving fifty-two examples of
lyrics and accompaniment. As the century proceeded, other
musical cards were issued, some with songs, some with dance
tunes, all of them now much coveted by collectors.

Before we get too involved in eighteenth-century England,
reference must be made to a popular subject on the Continent
in the seventeenth century—war. Two packs dealing with war
and defence were published first by Mariette in Paris, and then
by Daumont (1668 and c. 1710): these were Gilles de la
Boissière's *Jeu de la Guerre* and the *Jeu des Fortifications*. Both
were so popular that the designs were pirated in other countries.
They differ a little in form but basically one pack illustrates and
describes the events and situations of war (even to the enrol-
ment of troops) and the other illustrates the various types of
fortress and fortification. Curiously enough, from the number
of editions, Europe appears to have been more interested in its
defence than the possibility of waging a victorious war.

I have already mentioned some geographical packs in passing.
The fact that the seventeenth-century world appeared to com-

prise four continents made their distribution among the four suits quite irresistible to most cardmakers. Otherwise the form of the cards differed widely from pack to pack. Some merely listed nations and statistics, some provided maps, some showed pictures of inhabitants, and so on. Desmarests' *Jeu de Géographie*, for example, depicts a symbolic figure (representing a country) standing over a short description of the place. One pack omits suit-marks altogether, although four series of cards, each representing a continent, are numbered 1–10 and J, Q, K. (England, seventeenth century). Four packs obviously having a common origin were issued almost simultaneously in England, France, Germany and Italy in about 1675: these also assigned one suit to one continent, and according to the value on each suit listed that number of characteristics of each country. (See plate III.) In France in the following century another type of geographical card seems to have enjoyed a vogue, on which the names of areas take the place of suit-marks and the value is shown by a number of towns in a certain part of that area. A number of these cards must have been issued—probably about a dozen different packs—but few complete packs have survived. Perhaps the earliest known geographical pack was published in England: made in 1590 it depicted the counties of England and Wales (taken from Saxton's Atlas) under the four suit-names of East, West, North and South. Facsimiles of some of the cards were issued in sheet form by the Royal Geographical Society.

Geographical cards remained popular for many years although the nineteenth century saw a decline in their numbers; could it be that the discovery of a fifth continent upset cardmakers' ideas of design? Most eighteenth-century examples included maps in the design, but an exception appeared in 1790 with the arrival of the *Compendium of Geography* which was neither attractive nor interesting artistically but which contained a mine of information as to the late eighteenth-century view of the rest of the world. Every card is covered with instruction in some of the smallest type imaginable, the value being shown merely by a suit-mark and figure or letter in the top left-hand corner. Particularly interesting are the comments on the then recently lost colonies in North America.

There are, of course, instances where the two chapters covering pre-1800 and post-1800 cards must needs overlap slightly. Hodges' geographical cards and astronomical cards of c. 1828 really belong to the fashion of the previous century. Musical cards also appeared in both eras. Lenthall's fortune-telling cards were issued fifty years before the subject became a craze in France. But, generally speaking, with the French Revolution and the accompanying changes in class structures and political outlooks, and the rise of a new class during the Industrial Revolution, old card forms made way for new. It was almost as though a classical education was giving way to learning through journalism: even cards artistically designed usually had some form of gimmick to catch the interest, whether it was the ingenuity of caricature or portrayal of *haute couture*.

Pre-1800 cards are all difficult to find. Some are very expensive when they are found, particularly if they are in complete packs. Even single cards of many of the packs are worth having and never forget that many old cards were issued in more than one form: look in print shops for sheets of cards, and in booksellers' for those in book form.

The following list may not often be of use but it is designed to be of assistance when any really old (usually engraved) cards are found and are proving difficult to identify. Cards often turn up with an inadequate description or none at all, and it is very tantalizing to have no clue as to what they might be. The list cannot be complete, but it contains most of the more celebrated packs which have survived in varying quantities.

Clearly it would be of little practical use to the collector to try to make a wholly comprehensive list of such cards—many packs must have had so little success that one printing was quite enough and only single packs have survived. It is immensely satisfying for a collector to find a really old pack hitherto unknown, but he is more likely to come across those which enjoyed reasonable publicity and widespread sale. I therefore propose to list mainly those which enjoyed a certain contemporary reputation and particularly those which were advertised for sale by Lenthall of London in about 1717, by Mortier of Amsterdam at the same period, and certain other packs which were probably inspired by these cards and the early Desmarests packs. Lenthall does not, however, deal with the satirical propaganda packs of the second half of the seventeenth century in England, and I think a short description of these would be useful. Later cards which have attained a similar degree of celebrity are also described.

First of all, then, the four Desmarests packs, first issued in 1644, and all instructive in content, which influenced cardmaking for over a century.

Jeu des Rois de France. First issued in 1644 but reprinted in Paris as late as 1698. It is known in book form, sheet form, with or without suits, with forty cards (the original edition) or fifty-two cards. It was engraved by Stefano Della Bella and the following are its identifying characteristics. Each card depicts one or more of the kings of France with his name and description underneath. The kings of each suit are, in the opinion of the inventor, the greatest: hearts = *Louis le grand*, spades = *Charlemagne*, diamonds = *Henry le grand*, and clubs = *Clouis le grand*. Less aggressive, but possibly wiser or more virtuous, the monarchs shown on the queen cards are *Louis le Juste* ('*Pieux juste, chaste . . .*'), *Robert* ('*Pieux, sage, résolu . . .*'), *Sainct Louis* ('*Pieux, équitable, chaste . . .*') and *Pharamond* ('*Bon et sage Prince . . .*'). The headings given to those appearing on the jack cards are '*Malheureux*', '*Fayneants*', '*Simples*' (one of these, *Philippe* '*dit le long . . . souffrit toutes choses pendant son règne*') and '*Cruels*'. The values are shown by single suit-marks plus an arabic numeral or letter R, D, VA on the courts.

Jeu des Reynes Renommées. Similar in format to the preceding pack, but dealing with queens of many different countries and periods. Also known in several forms and reprinted in 1698. The idea for this pack was plagiarized by Mortier of Amsterdam, and it was also copied in Italy and Germany. In 1887 this pack was reproduced and presented to lady guests at the

Summer Meeting of the English Worshipful Company of Makers of Playing Cards. The value of each card is shown by a single suit-mark at the top and an arabic numeral or R, D, VA. The king cards all have the adjective *Saincte* written at the top right corner, and each of the other values is similarly devoted to a vice or virtue: the queens are *célèbre*, the jacks *vaillante*, aces are *heureuse*, 3s *capricieuse*, 6s *impudique* and 8s *cruelle*. We learn many curious facts from the descriptions of the ladies, their individual prowess often appearing quite startling.

Jeu de Géographie. First edition 1644 but reprinted up till 1698. Copied in Germany in at least two different versions with German suits and one was also issued with designs reversed. As in the case of the *Rois de France* this pack is known in several forms. Symbolic figures representing each country are depicted standing over a caption giving an account of the same. Countries of Europe are listed on hearts, of Asia on spades, of Africa on diamonds and America on clubs: an example of the type of caption to be expected: 8 of hearts—'*Grande Bretagne: Grande Isle, separée de la France par l'ocean vers le Septentrion, comprend L'Angleterre et L'Escosse, au couchant elle a l'Irlande, une autre grande Isle. Villes, Londres, Oxford, Douvres. Riv. la Tamise'.* The values are indicated by a suit-mark and arabic numeral or R, D, VA at top left.

Jeu des Fables. In common with the three preceding packs, this is known in several states and editions. It also clearly inspired N. de Fer's and Mortier's packs which are both called *Jeu des Metamorphoses d'Ovide* (see page 147). Each card shows mythological figure or scene at top and short legend underneath. Suit-mark and value at foot of the card. *Amphion* appears on the ace of spades, *Jupiter et Ganymede* on the 6 of hearts and *Pigmalion* on the 8 of spades. Copied in Germany.

Pl. V. Transformation cards of various periods. *Top and centre right:* two out of three known versions of the same joker; from *top* an unidentified pack (not Fuller's but possibly Jones') and *centre*, Cowell's of about 1810. *Top left:* from S. W. Fores' pack (1808). *Centre left:* hand-drawn original of about 1880. *Lower left:* Tiffany's 'Harlequin' (1879); *right:* a court card from Cotta's 'Wallenstein' pack of 1807.

N. de Fer's *Jeu des Metamorphoses d'Ovide* appeared in Paris in 1705, but is distinguishable by depicting more fussily engraved and detailed scenes of mythology over an account of same. The cards are numbered 1–52 as well as having suit-mark and number. Number 1 is the ace of spades and portrays Bacchus. The pack is known in sheet form complete with rules for play.

Heraldic cards are mentioned in both Lenthall's and Mortier's lists, and it is probable that both were referring to some edition of the Brianville cards. These had first been made in Lyons in 1658, under the direction of C. Oroncé Finé, M. de Brianville, and they ran to so many editions that it seems that they deserve a few paragraphs to themselves, as they were known on their own account for so many years both before and after the lists were issued. (I have also included some other celebrated contemporaries in this category.)

The form of design taken by these cards remained virtually constant throughout their life and was close to the two cards illustrated on plate II. The heart suit, with one or two exceptions, showed the coats-of-arms of the royalty and nobility of France, spades those of Germany and Scandinavia, diamonds those of Spain and clubs those of Italy.

The values are shown by single suit-marks at the top with a letter or figure. The courts are king, queen and prince, and the aces are called cavaliers. In the English pack, in order to place England in a suitably prominent position (she appears in most versions in the German arms suit of spades) the hearts and spades have had their designs transposed. In the Spanish pack Spanish suit-marks are used and cups represent Germany, swords Spain, money Italy and clubs France. An interesting difference in detail in this latter pack is that whereas elsewhere the king of France holds special pride of place as king of hearts, with an elaborate canopy placed over his coat-of-arms which

---

Pl. VI. *Top row from left:* typical eighteenth to nineteenth century Belgian tarot card; knight by Göbl of Munich; standard double-headed Empire court of early nineteenth century (from same pack as card at centre below). *Centre left:* non-standard Empire court. *Bottom left:* non-standard Empire satirical political pack of 1848. *Centre right:* standard Belgian animal tarot (c. 1830). *Bottom right:* Hungarian rebus pack of 1834.

has two page-like figures supporting it, this elaborate para-phernalia in the Spanish pack is accorded to the king of Spain.

The easiest method of placing the date of these cards is by the arms on the Pope's card, the king of clubs or money, which changed with the accession of each new Pope. Indeed, whole packs were made from re-engraved plates, but this method of dating is still the simplest. The following list of editions that I have so far discovered is therefore made with reference to the relative pontifical reign. (My descriptions are those of a lay person, not a herald.)

Alexander VII, 1655–67. His arms are divided in four quarters, the top left and bottom right showing an oak tree and the other two six hillocks surmounted by a star. During his reign the cards seem only to have appeared in France. The first edition in 1658, the second in 1660 and the third (known also in book form) in 1665.

Clement IX, 1667–69. His arms are also divided in four quarters, each quarter containing a lozenge or diamond shape. Another French edition appeared in this period; an English version and also a German edition are known too.

Clement X, 1670-76. Six solid-looking stars make a distinctive blazon. Valk of Amsterdam issued a copy of the French pack at this period, but without the written captions.

Innocent XI, 1676–89. A slightly more complex shield: the whole is made up of five horizontal lines, on the bottom of which are set three shallow cups or chalices, on the next two such cups, on the next one cup, on the next a leopard and on the top one an eagle. During this time a Lyonnais bookseller called Bulifon who had settled in Naples arranged publication in pack and book form of the first Italian edition of the cards in 1677, and another edition in 1681. A further French edition appeared around 1680.

Innocent XII, 1691–1700. His shield bears a picture of three pots. A further Italian edition appeared in 1691 in book and pack form, and in Holland that famous pirate of French playing cards, Mortier, brought out a copy of the French edition. He had also brought out a book describing the cards and giving a history of their subjects: this ran to at least eight editions. Bulifon also issued such a book.

Benedict XIII, 1724–30. The bottom half of his arms is taken up with broad diagonal bars. At the top a serpent crawls over a field of gold under a star-like rose. Mortier produced a further French edition in Amsterdam and another Italian edition appeared in about 1725.

Clement XII, 1730–40. His shield shows broad diagonal bars with a horizontal band across the centre. So far as I know the Spanish edition was the only one to appear as late as this. Although no subsequent edition of the cards is known to me, a descriptive book appeared in Madrid in 1748.

In England in 1675 there appeared a pack of a somewhat different character issued by Richard Blome. This, instead of concentrating on specific coats-of-arms, gives instruction in the art of heraldry. In fact, a book appeared in 1685, written by Blome, entitled *The Art of Heraldry* and using many of the illustrations which appear on the cards. The sub-title to the book is a lengthy one, but I quote part of it: '. . . Concisely Comprehending all necessary Rules in the said Art, with many useful Examples of Bearing, to facilitate the way of Blazoning any Coat of Armor . . .' This is virtually a description of the cards themselves: a large shield is placed in the top left of each card giving examples of a particular aspect of heraldry. For example, on the queen of diamonds various 'Beasts, or four footed Animalls' are displayed in various poses—'a Elephant passant . . . a stagg lodged . . . a grey hound currant . . . a bear rampant' and so on. The heading to each subject appears on the right of the shield under the value which is shown by a suit-mark at top right plus a roman numeral or half-length naturalistic court figure. Most of the heart suit, however, deal with examples of heraldry as practised among various ranks, and range from the 10 'The Atchivement of an Esquire, wch is the same as a Gentlemans' to 'His Ma^{tys} Royall Atchivement' on the king. The descriptions of all shields are fairly lengthy and appear on the lower part of each card. This pack was reproduced in 1888 for presentation to members of the Worshipful Company of Makers of Playing Cards.

Arms of the English Peers. 1677. This English pack is described in a contemporary advertisement as 'Cards containing the arms of the King and all the Lords Spiritual and Temporal of England'. This pack has a quite different format from the Blome pack and shows a number of shields on each card with the name and title of the holder underneath. The value is shown by a suit-mark plus arabic numeral or K, Q, P in the top left corner of each card. 1–4 of each suit, plus the 5 of clubs, is devoted to the arms of barons, the 5s of the other suits and the 6s of spades, diamonds and clubs to bishops, 6 of hearts and 7s of spades and clubs to viscounts and so on up the scale to the royal family. There were at least three editions (1677, 1686 and 1688). A distinguishing feature of the first was the coats-of-arms of Prince Rupert on the queen of diamonds and the Duke of York on the queen of hearts. In the third edition, on the queen of clubs under dukes, the Duke of Berwick has been added; on the 8 of clubs on the other hand, the Earl of Macclesfield's arms have been deleted. On the 9 of spades the garter has been placed round the shield of the Earl of Strafford.

Arms of the Scottish peers. c. 1691. Made in Edinburgh by a goldsmith, Walter Scott. This pack has a rather similar format to the last although, naturally enough, not so many coats-of-arms are displayed. The values are shown in the same fashion except that *King*, *Queen* and *Prince* are written out in full. 'Lords' take the place of 'Barons' on the lower value pip cards. The arms of Scotland, France, Ireland and England appear on the kings, those of the dukes of Hamilton, Gordon, Queensberry and Lennox on the queens. Reproductions of these cards appeared in the catalogue of the Edinburgh Heraldic Exhibition of 1891.

In 1693 a heraldic pack with a format similar to that of Brianville's was issued in Nuremberg showing the arms of the reigning houses of Europe, but with no similarity in arrangement. The inscriptions are in German. On the 2 of clubs are the Swiss cantons, and on the 3 the 'Hertzog von Modena'.

Silvestre's Heraldry. Made in Paris and issued first by Mariette in the late seventeenth century and reissued at the beginning of the next century by Daumont. It was copied in Germany in a curious form, all the designs being reversed—a death-blow to accurate heraldry; and, again in Germany, by Philipp Ernst Kieni of Augsburg with both German and French inscriptions. It is known in both card form and sheet form, the latter giving instructions for the game. The earlier editions of the sheets have written at the foot '*A Paris chez J. Mariette rue St. Jacques aux Colonnes d'Hercule avec privilege du Roy*'. On later sheets the address is changed to '*chez Daumont rue St. Martin*'. On each card, examples of heraldic art are shown in the form of shields with a description above and, where applicable, the name of the holder underneath. The value is shown by a single suit-mark usually placed at the top centre of the card plus the number of shields shown on the card. For example, on the 2 of diamonds there are two shields, the top one with '*Massoné ombré*' above it and '*Fortia*' underneath, the lower one with '*Massoné de 7 pièces*' and '*Marillac*' under it. The courts show symbolic figures and carry a general description of the honour it is to bear arms. Dedicated to the Duke of Burgundy.

In 1692 Thomas Almaury of Lyons issued a highly distinctive pack of heraldic cards designed by Père Menestrier using as suit-marks fleurs-de-lis (French nobility), roses (Italian), lions (Spain and Portugal) and eagles (Germanic states). The value of the pip cards is indicated by the number of shields thereon. For example, on the 10 of roses under the heading '*Ducs*' appear the 10 shields of the dukes of (the spelling is as on the card) *Mantove, Urbin, Parme, La Mirandola, Savoye, Medicis, Modene, Milan, Montferrat, Monaco*. On the fleurs-de-lis cards there are such headings as '*Chevaliers dv St. Esprit*' (*Messrs. de St. Simon, de Chaunes and de Villars*), '*Gentilshommes de la Chambre*', '*Chanceliers*' and so forth. The court cards show engraved portraits of contemporary European royalty and nobility.

Another fancy-suited pack *Preggi della Nobilita Veneta abboz-zati in un giuoco d'Armi di tutte le Famiglie. Di D. Casimiro Freschot.* This, in fact, may only be known in book form although it achieved at least two editions—the first in 1682 and the second in 1707. The suits are violets, roses, lilies and tulips —which makes them easy to identify. The pip cards all show seven coats-of-arms of Venetian families, but the court cards cover a wider field, and include other Italian dukes, the Elector of Bavaria, king of France, etc. The value is shown by a figure (arabic) or letter overprinted on a single suit-mark in the top right corner. (2–10 and R, D, P, C.)

John Lenthall, and his successors, published and sold playing cards for many years, probably beginning in the early 1660s and, from the evidence in the following list which is the most comprehensive of his surviving advertisements, continuing until at least 1717. Doubtless in his early days he sold the series of political-satirical cards which I have listed on pages 151–5 but by the date of this list such cards were either unfashionable or out of print. The only exception to this rule would appear to be the pack dealing with the events of the Spanish Armada.

Here then is the list with some description of those of the packs I have been able certainly or probably to identify.

'For the Improvement of Gentlemen, Ladies, and others, in several Arts and Sciences, as well as the agreeable Diversion of CARD-PLAYING, there are Publish'd Forty entertaining Packs of Cards, curiously engraven on Copper-Plates. Sold by J. Lenthall, Stationer, at the Talbot against St. Dunstan's Church in Fleet-street, London, viz.

'I. Heraldry Cards, being Draughts of the Coats of Arms of all the Princes and States, with Directions for blazoning each Coat of Arms, whereby may be learnt the whole of that curious Art.' This is probably the English edition of Brianville's heraldic cards; the only English edition I have been able to trace was issued in c. 1668 (see page 130).

'II. Travelling Cards representing all the principal Nations of the World, and the Habits of each Country, with Prospects of the capital Cities belonging to each Government, also Observations of the Fruitfulness, Religion and Trade. Design'd by the late ingenious Mr. Winstanly. With a Book of the Use of the Cards.' Mr H. Winstanley of Littlebury, Essex, first made this pack of cards in 1670 and promised to include on his cards as much information as 'Could be Contained in so Small a Space'. This he contrived to do by lengthy captions on the lower part of the card, engraved minutely. The upper half of the cards show a human figure and view of the country described, and each suit has an additional symbol and represents one continent: Tudor rose plus heart = Europe, moon plus spade = Africa, sun plus diamond = Asia, and star plus club = America. The value is shown by a single suit-mark plus numeral. The kind of subject matter found in this pack is exemplified by the ace of hearts: a regal figure stands outside a great city and the caption runs:

EUROPE

'Europe is the Least of the four Parts of the World and yet is not much Inferior to Any at this Present for containing Many Nations Most Polished and ingenuous (sic), where Arts and Sciences flourish and are Cherished, Trading abounding and Conversation without Dangers . . .'
and so on for a further hundred words or so.

'III. *Navigation cards*, wherein is contain'd all the Battles at Sea, fought between the English and Spaniards in Queen Elizabeth's Reign, and the Names of the cheif Officers that commanded the English and Spanish Fleets, and the particular Days of every Sea Fight.'

This pack is better known to collectors simply as *The Spanish Armada* pack. It has a format similar to other political and anti-Catholic packs of the same period (round about 1680); a narrow panel at the top indicates the value, displaying a single suit-mark plus a numeral or, in the case of the court cards, a medallion portrait alongside the word 'king', 'queen' or 'knave' (the latter are shown as a bishop, two cardinals and a monk). Underneath appears an engraving of the events and personalities engaged in the war and, at the foot of the card in another narrow panel, a short caption is written. The king of hearts, for instance, is devoted to the Tilbury review: 'The Army of 1000 horse and 22000 foot, which ye Earle of Leicester commanded when hee Pitched his Tents at Tilbury'. Another pack having cards also concerned with the Spanish Armada is 'All the Popish Plots' (see page 152).

'IV. *Map Cards*, describing the 52 Counties of England and Wales, each Card being a distinct Map, shewing the Length, Breadth and Circumference of each County; the Latitude, situation, and distance from London, of the principal Cities, Towns and Rivers, both by the reputed and measur'd Miles. Also a Compass for the Bearing to every Town, and a Scale for mensuration of the Distances. With printed Directions of the Use of the Cards.'

This pack achieved great popularity and has survived in at least three different versions. The basic design shows a map in the centre of each card, the value in a narrow panel at the top of the card (single suit-mark plus roman numeral or medallion portraits on the courts: Charles II is king, Katherine of Braganza is queen and various representative figures from the lower social orders make up the jacks); and the relevant information appears at the foot. A description from one of the explanatory cards accompanying the pack is probably clearer than my own would be: 'The four Suites are the 4 parts of England, the 13 Northern Counties are Clubs, the Western are Spades, the Eastern are Hearts, and the Southern are Diamonds. in each Card you have a Map of the County, with the cheife Towns and Rivers, a Compas for the Bearings, and a Scale for Mensuration. there is also given the Length, Breadth and Circumference of each County, the Latitude of the Cheife Citty or Towne, and its Distance from London. First the Reputed and then the Measured Miles. by Esqr: Ogilby. with his leave we have incerted. there is also the Road from London to each Citty or Towne, the great Roads are drawn with a double line, the Other Roads a single line, as also the cheif Hills and other remarks . . .'

What was probably the first edition of this pack was issued with maps lacking the names of adjoining counties and having a single line as border to each card. The two other editions both have the names of these counties inserted, but whereas one pack has a single line surrounding the design, the other has a decorated border typical of several Lenthall packs. (See plate III). The first edition was issued in 1676 by Robert Morden.

'V. *Astronomical Cards*, teaching any ordinary Capacity to be acquainted with all the Stars, to know their place in the Heavens, their colour, nature and bigness; with a Book of their Use.' Several editions, from 1676–1717. On each card a constellation is named and mapped so as to indicate its 'place in Heaven, Colour, Nature and Bigness'. The value is indicated by a single suit-mark plus roman numeral or medallion portrait. The pack is easily distinguished from another astronomical pack issued in London by Spofforth and Sons in about 1830; the latter indicates values on the pip cards by placing the suit-marks in their standard positions over the astronomical maps: also the court cards depict figures of mythological gods and goddesses, including six after whom planets are named.

'VI. *Geographical Cards*, adorn'd with the Effigies of the most considerable Princes in Europe. They shew the Longitude and Latitude of every part of the World; the Number of Kingdoms, Countries, Provinces and other Divisions; laid out by that celebrated Geographer, Monsieur Sanson. With Directions of the Use of the Cards.'

This is a version of a pack which appeared with variations and several editions in England, France, Germany and Italy between the years 1675 and 1717. This particular one is probably the edition which has the distinctive decorated border of so many Lenthall cards and also shows its value by a miniature standard card in the corner. It is also known without the border but redrawn and with reversed portraits on the court cards. As far as I can discover, all other versions indicate value by a single suit-mark and a numeral or word. The basic design of the cards is arranged as follows: each suit represents one continent, hearts = Europe, spades = Africa, diamonds

= Asia, and clubs = America; the aces list the principal
divisions of each continent and the pip cards make a further
breakdown, dealing with the number of items relating to the
value of the card (e.g. on the 2 of hearts, Denmark has two
provinces; on the 9 of hearts the nine principal islands of the
Mediterranean are listed). The court cards show medallion
portraits either of royalty or less exalted inhabitants of the
continents they represent. The queen of clubs, recognizable
on some versions, though not on others, as Queen Elizabeth I,
reigns over Virginia, 'Pomeiok, Jamestown and other places'
on non-English packs, but on home ground she is allowed a
more imposing list of 'The English Plantations on, or near, the
continent of AMERICA'. One English version was probably
sold by H. Brome in London, the French by Pierre Du Val
and was dedicated to the Dauphin, and the German by Joh.
Stridbeck Jr. in Augsburg. I cannot trace the origins of the
Italian pack although it is the only version of the cards which
I have in my own collection (see plate III).

Another allied pack is Lenthall's IX; see below.

'VII. *Mathematical Cards*, wherein those Instruments are exactly delineated, and apply'd to their various Operations. With
a printed Book of their Use. By the late ingenious Mr. Tuttle.'

This must be one of the first advertising packs, for Mr Tuttle
was mathematical instrument-maker to the King. Made c. 1700,
each card is most artistically and elaborately engraved. A
miniature standard card is in the top right-hand corner and
there is a broad white panel at the bottom on which the
explanatory caption is written. The main part of the card
depicts various instruments in use and the name of the instrument or its user appears on an elaborately framed tablet. For
example: on the 10 of spades 'Tellescope—An instrument of
vast information to our Sences by being well applyed to
Astronomical. & many other Mathematical Instruments'. The
10 of diamonds shows a Bricklayer and his tools. The ace of
spades gives a list of 'bookes and Instruments for Navigation'.

'VIII. *Geometrical Cards*, containing full and plain Instructions for the speedy Attainment of that most useful and curious

Science; with a printed Book of their Use: Likewise, A Discourse of the Mechanick Powers. All contriv'd by the late ingenious Mr. Moxon.'

Each card depicts a geometrical or mechanical principle. The value is shown by a suit-mark and roman numeral at the top: courts are indicated by the words *King, Queen, Knave.* 1697.

'IX. *Cosmographical Cards,* or, the whole World describ'd; each Card being a compleat Map, neatly engraven, and corrected by the best Geographers, with the Compass for the Bearings.'

This pack has much in common with Lenthall no. VI (q.v.) including the medallion portraits on the courts although personalities vary. King Charles, Rhea Silvia and A Tartar are the court cards of the Europe suit; Motezuma (*sic*), Queen Mary (probably Henrietta Maria) and an Indian fill these places on the America suit. The value and name of territory appear in a panel across the top of the card, but the remainder of the card is devoted to a map instead of text.

'X. *Cookery and Pastry Cards,* with full Instructions how to Dress all sorts of Fish, Fowl, or Flesh, and the proper Sauces to each Dish and Directions how to raise paste for all manner of Pies, made plain to the meanest Capacity.'

Sad to say I have never seen this pack, with all its insulting promise.

'XI. *Carving Cards,* shewing the best manner of cutting up all sorts of wild and tame Fowl, Fish and Flesh; with a printed book of their Use. By Mr. Moxon.'

'All the Flesh of Beasts are rang'd among ye Suit of Harts, All the fowl among the Suit of Dymonds, All ye bak'd meats among the Suit of Spades, And all the Fish among the Suit of Clubs.'

And so it is: each cut or joint or beast or pie is drawn diagrammatically, showing how it should be carved. The pack is known with or without Lenthall's border. The value is shown by a single suit-mark and roman numeral or half-length figures on the court cards. An immensely rare and delightful pack. Published in several editions between 1677 and 1717.

'XII. *British Cards*, describing the whole Territories of Great Britain. By Mr. Moxon.' I cannot exactly identify this pack: c.f. no XIII.

'XIII. *Historiographical Cards*, wherein is exactly describ'd the Situation, Climate, Customs, Manners, and Commodities, of every County in England and Wales, with the natural and artificial Rarities.'

This is probably a pack by W. Redmayne issued first in 1676. It is a good deal rarer than No. IV ('Map Cards') and presumably because of its more cumbersome design, enjoyed less success. The map of each county occupies a small part of the centre of a card and has the single suit-mark which denotes value almost obliterating the contours. The rest of the card is devoted to a description of the county: for instance, the queen of spades:

YORK-SHIRE

'The Greatest in all England, on the East is bounded with the German Ocean, on the West Lancashire and Westmorland, on the North with the Bishoprick of Durham, & on ye Sth wth Cheshire, Darby-shire, Nottingham-shire & Lincoln-shire. Its Temperate & Fruitfull, woods or Trees adorn it. The Citty is York, ye 2d Citty in all England. The Rivr. Ouse Runs through ye Citty, it hath a stone bridg. In it are 39 Great Townes & 459 Parishes, & in it are Excellent Rivers.'

The values are shown by numerals or half-length courts placed beside the central suit-mark. This pack might just possibly be No. XII and not XIII.

'XIV. *Grammatical Cards*, comprizing the general Rules of Lilly's Grammar, in the four principal Parts thereof, viz. Orthographia, Etymologia, Syntaxis, Prosodia: very useful to all Persons who understand Latin; not only for recollecting their memories, but for the farther improvement of such as have made some progress in that Language; whereby they may easily perfect themselves therein.'

Made by John Seller, and known both with and without the decorated Lenthall border. On the latter pack the value is indicated by a miniature standard card but on the former it is shown by a single suit-mark at the top left and a roman numeral to the right, half-length figures appearing on the courts. Syntaxis is dealt with on the hearts, Prosodia on the diamonds, Etymologia on the clubs and Orthographia on the spades. First published 1676.

'XV. *Arithmetical Cards*, teaching the useful Art after the most plain and easy method.'

These cards are known with the Lenthall decorative border and give on each card a practical problem. Some may appear to modern eyes a trifle ghoulish: an example is the 5 of hearts.

'Multiplication

Quest 3d. Suppose a Malefactor is tyed to a Cart, and order'd to be whipt thro' 7 Streets in Each of which are 9 kennels and at Every Kennel to receive 12 lashes, How many Lashes will he receive in all—

$$\begin{array}{r} 7 \text{ Streets} \\ 9 \\ \hline 63 \text{ Kennels} \\ 12 \\ \hline 756 \text{ Lashes'} \end{array}$$

A miniature standard card in the top right-hand corner denotes the value. c. 1710.

'XVI. *Proverb Cards*, containing pleasant Devices, suited to the most witty English Proverbs.'

Made c. 1700. Many of the proverbs illustrated here are still familiar. Each is written out in a panel at the foot of the card and the illustration appears above. The value is indicated by a single suit-mark at top right with a roman numeral at left or written words King, Queen and Knave in centre. Examples of the subjects covered are:

10 of hearts: 'Neck or Nothing'

8 of clubs: 'Men and Dogs may go abroad but women and Catts must stay at home'

7 of spades: 'He that is hang'd shall nere be drown'd'

Another pack of 'Proverbs' appeared a few years later in England, but with proverbs given in French as well as English, and the value indicated by a miniature standard card at the top right. The 5 of spades is a typical sample: 'A Good Wife is the Workmanship of a good Husband'.

'XVII. *Delightful Cards*, wherein is contain'd the Humours of the Age, the several Figures in each Card explain'd by Two Verses at the bottom of the Card, being diverting and entertaining to Gentlemen, Ladies and Others.'

On the jack of diamonds a travelling quack is shown addressing a crowd:

'Give me your Gold cryes quack here's my pills,
You think for Cure, no, to Increase your Ills'

On the 3 of diamonds a moral little tale is told and illustrated:

'In every Station Virtue bright does Shew
The modest Sempstress scornes ye lustfull Beau'

Values are shown by a standard miniature card in the top left corner of each card. The format is similar to that of 'Love Mottoes' (see No. XXIV) but the cards are slightly smaller and more crudely engraved.

'XVIII. *Fortune-telling Cards*, pleasantly unfolding the good and bad luck attending human Life. With Directions of the Use of the Cards.'

I am fortunate enough to own a complete pack of these cards together with the instructions which to me are so complicated that their 'message' remains obscure. However, they must have appealed greatly to contemporaries, for they were in circulation from the first half of Charles II's reign until after the death of Queen Anne. The values are shown by a single suit-mark and roman numeral in a narrow panel at the top: the value of the courts is shown in the same fashion—i.e. XI, XII and XIII— but whereas under the value these cards portray famous people both real and mythical (Pharaoh, Clytemnestra, Proserpina, Cupid, Wat Tyler are some of them) the pip cards comprise the odd numbers having a zodiacal wheel under the name of a magician or scientist, and the even numbers having a list of 'answers' under a sybil's name. For example, Merlin and Dr Faustus head the wheels on the 1 and 3 of clubs, and S. Phrygia and S. Lybica head the answers on the 2 and 4 of the same suit. These cards are known with or without Lenthall's border.

'XIX. *Frost Fair Cards*, being a Description of the several Trades in Booths, exercis'd on the River Thames, during the late memorable Frost.'

No pack of these cards appears to exist although there is at the Guildhall in London a sheet showing some of the cards which were cut-outs from a large representation of the Frost Fair of 1716 (or a modified picture of an earlier Fair). Values are indicated by roman numerals and suit-marks at the top of each card.

'XX. *Instructive Cards*, for Children, teaching them to spell and read in a short Time.'

Apart from its obvious antiquity, this is one of the least interesting of Lenthall's cards. Probably made at the beginning of the eighteenth century, the value is shown by a rather crudely drawn miniature standard court at top centre and a suit-mark at right: pip values have the same suit-mark at right, but only a roman numeral at centre. An oval frame at the centre of the card contains either half a dozen different ways of writing a single letter of the alphabet or a simple moral precept: 'If you play Lay no more than you can freely give to the Poore' appears on the 7 of spades.

Simply drawn natural history subjects are used to decorate the rest of each card.

'XXI. *Royal Cards*, describing the glorious Victories and most illustrious Actions in the Reign of her late Majesty Queen Anne.'

Engraved by R. Spofforth in c. 1705, these might be described as Loyal rather than Royal. The order of events portrayed on the cards is indicated by a number (arabic) in a top narrow panel in between the suit-mark and the roman numeral denoting the value (or, on the courts, King, Queen or Knave). Card no. 1 is the ace of hearts: 'Her Mty Proclaim'd

Q of Eng. Scot. Fra & Ireland etc. March 8 1702'. The numbering follows no pattern in relation to the value of the cards and
no. 52 finishes up on the 4 of clubs: 'Mareshl. Tallard & other
French Genls. brot Prissonrs to England.' R. Spofforth engraved his name on that card although the caption was little
enough to boast about. The captions occupy a narrow strip
at the foot of the card and most of the space is taken up by the
central illustration.

Another pack, not mentioned by Lenthall, dealing with the
victories of Marlborough was issued a year or so later. It seems
to have been the work of several engravers and has a good deal
of elaborate detail. Some of the court cards portray half-length
figures of European royalty (Charles III of Spain on the king of
clubs, Queen Anne on the queen of clubs, George Prince of
Denmark on the king of hearts and so on). The value panel and
extra number have disappeared although values are still indicated by a single suit-mark and roman numeral or word. The
spade suit is devoted to blackening the reputation of Louis XIV
but most of the other cards deal extravagantly with the victories
of the Duke of Marlborough. A sample of the English view
of the French king is depicted on the queen of spades (see
plate III).

'XXII. *Forrest Cards*, representing all sorts of Birds and
Beasts: finely engraven and drawn to the Life with the Name of
each Bird and Beast.'

This extremely rare pack is known with a decorated Lenthall
border but has a most unusual format for the period, in that the
pip cards are full size and in their standard position, with
pictures of animals engraved as a background on the spades and
clubs and birds on the other two suits. Naturalistic but nondescript figures appear on the courts. This pack may have been

Pl. VII. Examples of non-standard cards. *At left, from top:* United States Civil
War pack; early nineteenth-century German 'hunting' pack; patriotic German
cards of about 1890. *Centre:* a Bohemian over-knave of toboggans (c. 1910) and
French Revolutionary 'element' of diamonds from about 1793. *Right, from top:*
from a series of French fashion plate packs (c. 1855); early nineteenth-century
Spanish ace of swords; modern Bohemian over-knave.

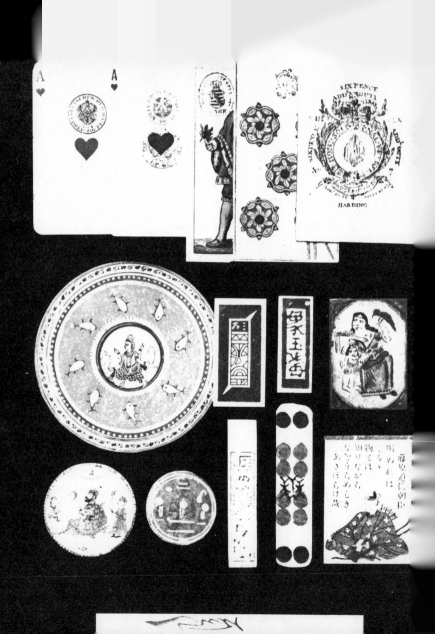

copied from a rather similar pack made earlier in the seventeenth century in Germany.

'XXIII. *Pastime Cards*, consisting of Morals, Precepts, Fancies and Tales.'

The above is a just description of this late seventeenth-century pack. A standard miniature card in the top left corner shows the value of each card. A lengthy caption appears in a broad panel at the bottom, and the rest of the card is devoted to illustration and a tablet for the title of the subject matter ranging from 'Quibbles' on the 3 of spades, to 'The Bacchanal or A Company of honest Hearts giving Nature a Phillip' on the 9 of spades.

'XXIV. *Love Cards*, or The Intrigues and Amusements of that Passion merrily display'd.'

Made c. 1710, this pack is similar in format to the *Pastime Cards* but is more finely engraved and has some miniature standard cards top right and some top left. A rhyming couplet is given as caption to an illustration of some romantic situation although the philosophy concerning 'that Passion' is by no means all starry-eye'd in character: on the 7 of hearts we read 'When hearts are staked at ye odd game call'd Love, It's hard to guess which does the looser (*sic*) prove', and again on the 6 of spades: 'The Courtier truly knows the powerfull art to Dance a Lady's Honor from her heart'. See plate III.

Lenthall's list now moves on to the imported cards which he had for sale.

'The following Cards are explain'd in French; design'd for the more easy and expeditious Attainment of that language, viz.

Pl. VIII. *Top:* tax stamps. *From left:* German Empire prior to 1918; Czech Republic and German stamps of the 1920's; Saxon stamp of 1855; eighteenth-century Austrian 'G' Graz); typical English eighteenth and nineteenth-century spade ace—this is probably forged. *Below:* cards of Asia; *left:* variations in size and style from India; 8 of fishes from 10-suit pack, two kings of sun from luxury and 'bazaar' packs. South-eastern Asian and Chinese cards at *centre*; *at right:* Persian and Japanese cards with Korean below.

'XXV. *Fortification Cards*, teaching that whole Art according to the newest Method, as practis'd by the best Engineers with a Book of the Use of the Cards.'

This pack must be the *Jeu des Fortifications* first issued in Paris in 1668 and later in c. 1710. Mortier of Amsterdam (who, I suspect, supplied Lenthall with his foreign cards) advertised himself as selling a *Jeu des Fortifications* but I do not know if this was advertising an example of his own piracy or whether he in turn had imported the cards from Daumont in Paris. I know of one edition pirated in Amsterdam, but this was a German-language edition by Peter Schencken entitled *Das Festung Baues Spiel*. Another German edition is also known, and also a 48-card version with Spanish suits entitled *Juegos de la Fortification*.

A miniature card in the top right corner gives the value and to its left appears a heading and lengthy caption describing an aspect of the science of fortification. Underneath, the system referred to is illustrated either as a general picture or a detailed plan. For example, a picture of a 'Chateau' is represented on the 10 of hearts, the plan of a 'Contregarde' is on the 7 of spades. The pack is also known in sheet form.

'XXVI. *Military Cards*, being a description of Battles, Sieges, etc., containing Rules for attaining a compleat knowledge in the Art of War, with a Book of the Use of the Cards.'

This is the companion pack to, indeed the forerunner of, the Fortification Cards, and is the *Jeu de la Guerre* invented by Gilles de la Boissière, first published by Mariette in 1668 and later by Daumont. It has a different format from the Fortification Cards, but much the same printing history (on sale in Amsterdam, published in German in Amsterdam with reversed designs, published in Germany, etc.) but I cannot trace a Spanish edition. In German it is called *Das Kriegs-Spiel*.

Each card contains in its upper half an energetic illustration of some stage of war—bombardment, encampment and so forth. Underneath is a long caption explaining the situation or procedure. The value is indicated by a single suit-mark enclosing a roman numeral or letter in a top corner.

There were other packs besides these two on war-making in

the seventeenth century, although few were wholly devoted to the subject. One in the British Museum, however, comes from Germany, has German suit-marks and is devoted to the war between the Turks and Germans.

'XXVII. *Heraldry Cards*, being Draughts of the Coats of Arms of all the Princes and States in the World, whereby may be learn'd the whole of that curious Art.'

This would appear to be a French-language edition of Brianville's cards, but also might conceivably be an edition of the Silvestre/Mariette/Daumont heraldic cards (see page 132).

'XXVIII. *Poetical and Philosophical Cards*, containing the Effegies of the most antient Poets and Philosophers, taken from the most celebrated statues and medals.'

This may be the pack advertised by Mortier of Amsterdam as *Jeu des Hommes & Femmes Illustres* although it might at first seem unlikely. The latter pack shows bust portraits of famous classical figures on the top half of the card, with a background of narrow horizontal lines. The name and description in French is given underneath. The value is shown by a single suit-mark at top left with a numeral or letter. The 'C' (ace) of hearts is Aristophanes. Perseus is on the 10 of hearts and Annibal on the 7 of spades.

A pack made in Germany in 1685 by Johann Stridbeck of Augsburg, with medallion portraits and descriptions of philosophers, poets, warriors and other celebrities, would seem to come closer to Lenthall's description but I cannot trace it in other than a German edition, unless Mortier's cards are in fact copied from the idea.

'XXIX. *Chronicle Cards*, representing the Effigies of all the Kings of France, with a summary Account of the Reign of each Monarch.' Probably a late edition of the Desmarests *Jeu des Rois de France*. See page 127.

'XXX. *Ladies Cards*, or the Glory of the Female Sex illustrated in the Lives of heroical Women of all Nations eminent for their Valour and Virtue, with their Effigies finely engraven.'

Likewise, probably a late edition of the *Jeu des Reynes Renommées*, see page 127.

'XXXI. *Classical Cards*, representing all the Fables in Ovid's Metamorphoses.'

This might be one of at least two packs: first N. de Fer's *Jeu des Metamorphoses d'Ovide* published in Paris in 1705: scenes from the legends are shown over an account of same. Each is numbered (1–52) as well as having suit-mark and numeral or letter. No. 1 is the ace of spades and depicts Bacchus. The other pack was issued by Mortier and also called *Jeu des Metamorphoses d'Ovide* but has a different format, the captions being engraved on a draped tablet at the foot of the card. Values are shown on a single suit-mark with numeral or letter (R, D, P and C for ace) at the top centre of the card. The engraving is not so delicate as that on the Fer pack. The king of hearts shows Momus, the queen Jupiter and the jack Juno.

'XXXII. *Historical Cards*, describing the Cities and most remarkable Places in the World, with the Habits peculiar to each Country exactly delineated.'

This is probably the late edition of the *Jeu de Géographie* described on page 128.

'XXXIII. *Roman Cards*, representing the lively Effigies of the Roman Emperors and Empresses, with a Summary of their Exploits; also a Chronological History of the Kings of France, under the Effigies of each Monarch, curiously engraved.'

Probably the pack described on Mortier's list as *Jeu des Rois de France*, for a pack is known, engraved by the Dutch engraver J. Gole (see also XXXV and XXXVI) with medallion portraits of the French kings, sometimes two for each card, over an account of their reigns on the pip cards, while the courts show some imperial Roman personalities (*Octave Auguste* on the king of clubs) although *Scaramouche* appears on the jack of spades. Charlemagne is depicted on the 10 of spades, Charles Martel on the ace of clubs; c. 1704.

'XXXIV. *Geographical Cards*, describing in exact Maps, all Parts of the World, drawn from the latest Discoveries.'

Probably Mortier's *Jeu de Géographie*. Each card shows the map of one country; there is a reference scale at the foot and title of map at the top. Value shown by suit-mark at top. This must be very similar to a host of geographical packs issued in the eighteenth century: in an ever-expanding world the subject of geography was extremely popular with cardmakers, and I describe a few which do not appear on this list, on pages 157–161.

'XXXV. *World Cards*, representing in Figures, finely delineated, the 12 Months, and 4 Seasons of the Year, the 5 Senses, the 4 Elements, the several liberal Arts, the 4 Parts of the World, and other Curiosities.'

This is almost certainly Mortier's *Jeu des quatre parties du Monde*, engraved by J. Gole. It has a small format and the value of the pip cards is shown by a miniature, borderless, standard card at top right or left. The courts (which show a variety of people on medallion portraits) have merely a suit-mark plus the words 'Roy Koning', 'Reine' or 'Le Valet'. All other cards depict a female figure, each one differently dressed and with a different occupation, with a caption at the foot of each card in French. The respective numerals of each suit are related: 10s = continents, 9s = the Elements, 8s = the time of day, and so on.

'*The following Cards are explain'd in Dutch and French, viz.*

'XXXVI. *Masquerade Cards*, representing the various and most artful Disguises us'd at those Diversions.'

It seems likely that this is Mortier's *Jeu de Boufon*. This is probably another pack engraved by J. Gole, and one which is known in both large and small format—probably the first known instance of the same cards being issued in two sizes, although the smaller pack is less well engraved and not signed by J. Gole. The card shown in plate III is typical of the format of the pip cards, each portraying a different character, ostensibly from the *Commedia dell'Arte*. The kings and queens depict full-length portraits of the reigning monarchs of England (William and Mary), the Empire (Emperor and Empress), France (Louis XIV and '*Madame de Mintenon*' on the large pack and '*La Reine de France*' on the small one) and Spain, while lesser mortals take the part of the jacks. The titles on the pip cards are in Dutch, the captions on the courts in French. The pack in the British Museum has four extra jacks, all harlequins, but the style of engraving seems quite different, and it is not clear why they should have been added: c. 1690.

I have been unable to identify or trace the remainder of the cards on the list although there is evidence that in Germany too there was a vogue for cards depicting the fashions of various localities.

'XXXVII. *Scaramouch Cards*, containing the many Ways of distorting the Body and Limbs, us'd by the most expert Dancing Masters.

'XXXVIII. *Entertaining Cards*, describing the Fashions of most nations.

'XXXIX. *Turkish Cards*, shewing the several Customs us'd, and Habits worn, by People of all Degrees in that Nation.

'XL. *Habit Cards*, representing the Dresses worn in Holland and in Augsburg, by Persons of all Ranks.'

As an appendix to Lenthall's list the following is a list of cards advertised as being available from 'J. Covens and C. Mortier' in Amsterdam at about the same time.

'*Jeu d'Armoiries* (see Lenthall XXVII)
Jeu des quatre parties du Monde (XXXV)
Jeu des Rois de France (XXXIII)
Jeu des Hommes & Femmes Illustres (XXVIII)
Jeu des Reines Renommées (XXX)
Jeu des Metamorphoses d'Ovide (XXXI)
Jeu de Géographie (XXXIV)
Jeu des Fortifications (XXV)
Jeu de la Guerre (XXVI)
Jeu de Boufon (XXXVI)'

Just how many of these were originals by Mortier of Amsterdam, how many were pirated ideas and how many were genuine importations from Paris is difficult to judge, but clearly there were strong trade links between the card publishers of England and Holland, probably following the Revolution.

The category most obviously missing from both these packs

is the political propaganda series. The Spanish Armada pack, obviously originally intended as part of a series of anti-Catholic cards, is played down by Lenthall as being 'Navigation Cards'. However, there were plenty of topical dislikes to inflame in the second half of the seventeenth century, and the cards which resulted continued to be issued until the fall of the Stuart monarchy.

Although, to begin with, this type of political card was an English phenomenon, it seems likely that the form the cards took was inspired by the instructive packs issued in France in the 1640s. Very few fragments of English cards from before the time of Cromwell have survived, but from those which have there is very little evidence that cards were used for any purpose but diversion. Following the Restoration in 1660, however, the first use of cards as a vehicle for political and religious propaganda is apparent. Probably the first pack issued was no. 1 below, which satirized the Commonwealth government, but most of the others published prior to 1700 were devoted to vicious attacks on Roman Catholicism.

Most of the cards have a similar format: the card is taken up with engraved illustration over a caption of varying length, and the value is nearly always shown by a single suit-mark in the panel at the top, plus a number and letter or word.

1. *The Rump Parliament* or 'A complete political satire of The Commenwealth'. The origins of this pack are uncertain, although one theory is that they were in fact made in Holland during Charles II's exile. Certainly very few examples of the pack have survived in its original form. It is composed of a series of satirical, scurrilous and abusive pictures of the Rump Parliament and its Commonwealth successors. The ace of clubs shows a private house being sacked, and a lady being abducted, with the caption 'A Free state or a tolleration for all sort of Villany'. The ace of spades has the caption 'Bradshaw, the Iaylor and ye Hangman, keepers of the Liberty of England'. The 10 of clubs shows Oliver Cromwell praying with an execution taking place in the background: 'Oliver seeking God while the K. is murthered by his order.' The queen of

spades has the caption 'The Lady Lambert and Oliver under a strong Conflict' and shows this couple seated together on a bed.

In 1885 Edmund Goldsmid, honorary secretary of the Aungervyle and Clarendon Historical Societies, published a book entitled *A Pack of Cavalier Playing Cards* which included facsimile illustrations of this pack. A facsimile pack was issued round about the same time and, although scarce, is the collector's best chance to own a likeness of a most interesting commentary. Unfortunately, two cards were missing from the pack illustrated: these two, the ace and 3 of hearts, were, as Mr Goldsmid put it, 'supplied from another source'. It happened to be the wrong source, but whether the cards came from another pack of the same period (not known to me) or whether they were artistic figments of a nineteenth-century imagination I have not yet been able to discover. The substituted cards are also anti-Cromwell.

There is unlikely to be confusion between two packs produced in the seventeenth and nineteenth centuries respectively, but, as a matter of interest, I give the relevant captions of the cards concerned:

	Original version	Aungervyle facsimile
ace	A Comitte of Godwin Nye Peters and Owen discovering the marks of grace in Ministers	Cromwell, Ireton and Hudson all in ye same Boate
3	Sr. Gilbert Gerard and his two souns	Cromwell pypeth unto Fairfax

The values are shown in the top panel by a single suit-mark on the left and a roman numeral on the right. The courts are inscribed King, Queen, Knave.

2. *All the Popish Plots*. Of the following packs which express anti-Catholic sentiments, *The Popish Plot* was by far the most popular. I am, however, listing *All the Popish Plots* first, as it covers some of the same ground dealt with in other packs.

The Spanish Armada pack has, of course, already been described on page 135, but the subject is also dealt with in the pack under discussion. The illustrations include the Queen inspecting the Army of Foot at Tilbury (the ace of hearts) and on the king she 'makes an oration to her Army upon the defeat of the Spanish Armada'. On the 4 of hearts a sinisterly familiar caption runs 'The King of Spain onely treats of Peace but makes greater Preparations'. On the 9 of hearts 'Sr. F. Drake takes a great Gallion and in it Don Pedro with 40 Nobles of Spain and 55000 Duckets in Gold'. On the 10 of clubs 'The Spaniards bring Torches Whips of Whipcord and Wire and Butchers Knives to Murther and torture the English'.

Other plots illustrated are the Gunpowder Plot, Dr Parry's Plot against Queen Elizabeth, and the Titus Oates Plot. The 2 of spades claims to show 'Dr Parry consults some Persons to Poyson or Stab Q. Elizabeth'. The 10 of spades illustrates 'Guy Faukes brought to ye Council where he laments nothing but he had not Executed his designe'. The 2 of diamonds shows two assassins lying in wait: 'The Papists design to Murther Faukes in St. Georges fields if ye blow had been given and to lay ye Plot on the Protestants'. One or two of the captions appear on different cards in *The Popish Plot*, notably 'Pickerin attempts to kill ye king in St. Iames Park' (8 of diamonds in *All the Plots* and jack of diamonds in the other) and 'Sr. Edmondbury Godfree Strangled Girald going to stab him' (on 6 of diamonds in *All the Plots* and 9 of spades in the other). From the style of engraving it almost looks as though the diamond suit was engraved by a different person from the engraver of the other suits, possibly by the same man who executed the *Popish Plot* cards. The values are shown in the same way as on the preceding pack.

3. *The Popish Plot*. This was clearly the most popular of the anti-Catholic packs, possibly because the events portrayed thereon were more vivid in public memory. They deal primarily with Titus Oates, his plot and the subsequent murder of the magistrate Sir Edmondbury Godfree. The ace of hearts shows the Pope and his cardinals sitting round a table under which the Devil is seen crouching: 'The Plot first hatcht at Rome by the Pope and Cardinalls'. Most of the spade suit is devoted to the murder of 'Sr. E. B. Godfree' or 'Sr. E.B.G.'.

Examples of this pack are known made from four different sets of plates. Two of them are identical in format although the redrawing of detail is readily apparent: the values are shown by a single suit-mark and roman numeral or word at the top. On the third set the courts have medallion portraits to the right of the card: on the fourth pip cards' value is shown by a small panel in the top left only containing a suit-mark and roman numeral.

4. Made in about the same period (1678–80) was a pack dealing with an alleged plot found in a meal tub and organized by Mme Cellier, together with Dangerfield. The format is the same as for the first two plates of the Popish Plot, and on the 7 of clubs the caption reads 'The sham Plott discovered in the meal tub'. This rare pack is known as *The Meal Tub Plot*.

5. Another notorious plot portrayed on cards was *The Rye House Plot* which directed its wrath against the old Roundhead enemy. The plot was to murder the royal brothers on their way home from the Newmarket races and aroused an implacable rage amongst the ranks of the Tories who stopped at nothing in order to implicate as many enemies as possible in the plot. The format is as for the last packs. On the king of hearts appears the gloomy scene of 'E. of Essex cutting his throat in ye Tower'. The ace of spades shows 'Hone taken Prisoner at Cambridge'. The plot took place in 1683.

6. *The Reign of James II*. More anti-Catholic propaganda; the events of the reign include the flight of the king from the country in 1688. The ace of spades also involves his predecessor: '500 thousand pound sent from France yearly to Charles the 2 to keep the sitting of the Parlement of'. Here the indignation seems to have reached a stage of incoherence. The format is the same as for the last packs.

7. *The Duke of Monmouth's Rebellion*. Again the same format and again the anti-Stuart emphasis; issued in c. 1688. The invading Duke is frequently referred to in the captions as the Duke or D. of M. and should not be confused with the D. of Marlborough who appears in later packs. Many captures and executions are shown including the D. of M. himself (7 of

spades), Desny (jack of diamonds), 'Severall of ye Rebells . . .'
(5 of diamonds), Rombold the Maltster (10 of diamonds), Mme
Lisle (queen of hearts) and Argyle (3 of hearts). There is also a
great deal of fighting, looting, gibbeting, burning and whipping.

8. Came *The Revolution*. Some of the events shown are also
recorded on no. 7, but there is more concentration on the
qualities of William of Orange. The memory of other packs is
also evoked: the 3 of clubs shows 'Oates Whipt from Algate to
Tyburn'; the ace of clubs gives a different version of an incident
in the Rye House Plot—'The Earle of Essex's Throat Cut' (he
is also murdered on the nine of hearts in King James II's
Reign). There is a bloodthirsty sequence in which the Popish
midwife (who presumably could tell whether or not the 'Prince
of Wales' was the genuine heir) hacks her husband to pieces
(queen of clubs), puts 'his quarters in ye Privy' (ace of spades)
and finally burns at the stake (2 of spades). Both nos. 7 and 9
question the legitimacy of the royal baby: the 2 of diamonds
in no. 7 shows a four-poster with the curtains drawn and the
caption 'The Queen is brought to bed of a Boy—Reported so'.
In no. 9 an extra weapon of distaste is employed on the 10 of
spades: 'P of Wales baptized. Ye Nuncio stands Godfather for
ye Pope' and on 8 of spades the arrival of 'a consecrated smock'
for the child, delivered by cardinals.

This appears to be the first pack which, as well as having the
traditional method of indicating value, also includes in the top
panel a sequence of arabic figures, 1–52. The clubs have the
sequence 1–13, the spades 14–26, the diamonds 27–39 and
hearts 40–52. (See also Lenthall no. XXI on page 143.)

The age of protest by cardmaking was nearly over in England
and only showed a few signs of activity in the first decades of
the eighteenth century.

9. *The Impeachment of Dr Sacheverell*. The events of this
relatively unknown trial acted as a kind of climax to the Whig
policy and oppression. On the day commemorating the glorious
Revolution, the good doctor preached in Church a sermon
attacking its principles. The result was his impeachment by the
Lords, an act which fanned the will of the English people to

have a change of masters and to make peace with Europe. The Whigs and Tories had for some years concentrated on soliciting the support of the people by discussing and pamphleteering, and this encouraged the freedom of argument and opinion which is evident in this and the following two packs. This particular pack was one of the first to use the device of printing miniature cards in the top corner of each card to indicate value. Otherwise the formula of illustration and caption was maintained. Queen Anne was not unsympathetic towards the offender and one of the captions, that on the 9 of spades, runs 'Sentence upon offenders may be pass't / Yet Monarcks Pardon those whom Juryes cast'; c. 1710.

10. *All the Bubbles*. c. 1720. This delightful pack has much the same format as the last—a miniature card in the top left corner, an illustration and captions (in rhyming verses) but also a narrow panel at the top on which the name of the particular financial venture discussed is written. The pack portrays many of the abortive and prosperous schemes for making money attached to the notorious South Sea and other bubbles. I cannot resist quoting some of the very forthright opinions of the author of the cards.

7 of spades	You that delight to keep your Sweaty Feet
Stockings	By often changing Stockings Clean and Sweet,
	Deal not in Stockin Shares, because I doubt
	Those that buy most, e'erlong will go without.
6 of spades	Come all ye Gen'rous Husbands, with your Wives,
Insurance on	
Lives	Insure round Sums, on your precarious Lives;
	That to your comfort, when you're Dead and Rotten
	Your Widows may be Rich when you're forgotten.
5 of diamonds	Rare fruitfull Isles where not an Ass can find
Bahama Islands	A verdent Tuft or Thistle to his Mind!
	How then must those poor Silly Asses fare
	That leave their Native Land to Settle there?

See plate III.

11. *The South Sea Bubble.* c. 1720. This pack with a more specific target does not have the top panel for sub-titles on the cards. There is also a quantity of 'balloons' used in displaying the comments of the characters appearing on the cards as well as the lines of caption at the foot. The verses are often bawdy and sometimes incomprehensible. On one pack I have seen, certain captions have been scratched out by a later, more sensitive hand.

12 and 13. Two more Bubble packs, this time from Holland, also belonging to the year 1720. They are almost identical in illustration but differ in caption. One is the 'Kaartspel van Momus naar de Nieuwste Mode' and the other is entitled 'Pasquins Windkaart op de Windnegotie van 't Iaar 1720'. Each card shows an allegorical illustration of some unfortunate aspect of the Bubble troubles (in this case the main scheme criticized is the Mississippi scheme) and a rhyming caption in Dutch is placed at the foot of the card (see plate II). The value is indicated by a single suit-mark at top right of each card with an arabic number or word close by. (The courts are called Heer, Vrouw and Knegt.) I give below a few identifying differences between the two packs:

	Momus	*Pasquin*
king of clubs (inscription in illustration)	Bewindhebber van Na geluk druk	Eerst gelukkig Na drukkig
jack of hearts	Boeve Actien	Uit Wanhoop
9 of diamonds	De Grootste is Koning	Vor den Koning

14. Anti-Catholic cards came only belatedly to Holland and in c. 1719 an anti-Papal pack appeared which raked up all the old scandals that could be found. Even Pope Joan is shown on the 3 of hearts. The format is similar to the Bubble cards of Holland and is therefore easily recognizable. After this the political activities of cardmakers more or less lapsed for about a hundred years.

The principal eighteenth-century survivor of playing-card

trends from the previous century was the geographical pack. Large numbers of such cards were issued in England, France, Germany and Italy, some artistically designed, others unimaginative in format but interesting for the information they contain. The following is a representative list of the different types of card the collector might search for.

First, a rather irritating fashion for substituting areas for suit-marks. In the middle of the century about a dozen different packs appeared in France with this characteristic, obviously part of the same series. Each covers a certain area and the names of four regions in that area are substituted for suits. In one such pack the 'suits' are Burgundy, Provence, Dauphiné and Lyonnais and in another they are Austria, Bohemia, Silesia and Bavaria. Other packs dealt with other parts of Europe from Lithuania to Spain and Rumania to Ireland. The name of the suit is written at the top of each card and the value of the pip cards is indicated by the number of towns shown on a map of part of the region concerned. For example, the 3 of Orleanais shows the towns of Chatillon, Gien and Briare. The court cards show the heads of a king, queen and commoner peering over draped curtains inscribed with statistical details of the territory.

The *Giuoco Geografico dell'Europa* is rather similarly arranged; an Italian tarot pack probably made in Naples in c. 1770. The four 'suits' are here named *Nord, Sud, Centro* and *Isole*. Pip values are given in arabic numerals and the four courts in roman numerals, I-IV. The courts describe the countries of each region (on the *Centro* suit, for example, the countries involved are Germany, France, Poland and, on IV, Low Countries and Switzerland) and on the pip cards their subdivisions are listed. England is described on the I of *Isole* and its divisions listed on the 2: '1. *Del Nord* 2. *Dell'Est* 3. *Del Sud* 4. *Dell'Ouest* 5. *Di Galles* 6. *Di Mezzo*'. These regions had listed as their capital towns, respectively: 'Yorch Londra residenza del Re Contorbery Salysbery Montgomery Lincoln'. On another card Londorderi and Gallowai are found in Ireland. The trump cards show decoratively designed maps of European countries with their names on tablets at the top of the cards plus five maps of continents—America being divided into north and south—and a card depicting the Fool looking at the out-pouring of *Fiumi Principali di Europa*.

A geographical cum heraldic pack was issued in Bologna in 1725 in the form of a *tarocchino* pack and it, or its accompanying booklet, gave offence to the Papal authorities who demanded that the *Papi* cards (normally the Pope, Popess, Emperor and Empress) should henceforward be illustrated simply as Moors (see page 35). The value of the cards is shown by a truncated version of the *tarocchino* pack (and partly non-standard) in a narrow panel across the top of the cards. The trump cards are devoted to a geographical survey of the world. For example, on The Tower (depicted merely as a flash of lightning) a heading of *Le Principali Isole di tutto il Mondo* has under it two sub-headings 'The new world contains' and 'The old world contains' which in turn have sub-headings—'North America' and 'South America' for the former and 'Africa', 'Europe' and Asia' for the latter—and so on down to the names of individual islands. The cards belonging to the four suits display the heraldic shields of the Italian nobility.

Another pack from Italy, also fitting into the regional form, is a 52-card pack with miniature Venetian cards as values, issued by Giambattista Albrizzi in Venice in about 1779. This also lists the territories of the world, and each suit deals with one continent—cups = Europe, swords = Africa, money = Asia, and batons = America. The 3 of cups, for instance, deals with *'Gran Bretagna'* and lists the territories *Inghilterra propria, Il Principato di Galles, che insieme contengono* 52 *Provincie* . . . and the principal towns *Londra Cap del Regno, Cantorbery, Yorck, Oxfor*, etc.

Albrizzi also issued a more or less companion pack at the same time dealing with the History of the Popes: the 6 of swords unexpectedly tells us that Alexander VI (Borgia) sent missionaries to the New World and was responsible for the introduction of the Faith to the Congo and the Cape of Good Hope: nothing more. See plate II.

Another Italian pack (although with French inscriptions)

embracing substitution of areas for suit-marks was invented by L'Abbe Desprotti in Parma in 1790. The suits of swords, cups, clubs and money have been replaced respectively by maps of Italy, Germany, France and Spain respectively, while the trump cards '*designe la Sphere, la Terre et ses diverses parties qui sont a la place des Taroqus*'. This explanatory card took the place of the Fool. Values were indicated by roman numerals at the top of each card, and every card has *Nord, Sud, Ouest* and *Est* inscribed suitably on its four edges. Contemporary history is reflected in the fact that the 2 of Germany is a map of the British Isles under the Hanovers.

Back in England, as the century drew to a close, two rather drab-looking packs emerged containing a good deal of closely-set information. The first, published in 1790, was entitled 'A Systematical Compendium of Geography On the Face of 52 cards'. The value of each card is shown by a large suit-mark with reverse block numerals (arabic) or letters in the top left corner. The remainder of the card is packed with geographical information set in extremely small type. As in many other packs, each suit is devoted to a specific continent: hearts = Europe, spades = Asia, diamonds = America, and clubs = Africa. The name of each continent appears on the suit-mark of the aces. The courts give statistics of latitude, size, population, etc., of each country in the continent, and the remainder of the copy runs straight on, ace–10. The kingdoms of Europe, we learn from the king of hearts, 'excel in arts and in power; England is first, France Spain and Holland next'. On the 8 of diamonds the forecast is hazarded that 'probably to have a residence [N.W. of the Ohio] will be the highest state of luxury, within the course of a century or more'. On the 10 of diamonds it is stated that Brazil has 'inexhaustible treasures of silver and gold'. There were at least two editions of the pack: one has a thin black border surrounding each card; on the other a red border surrounds the hearts and diamonds and there is a small star at each corner of the border of every card.

The second pack was issued in London by J. Wallis in 1799 and entitled 'The Geography of England and Wales, accurately delineated on fifty-two cards, including the boundaries, extent, products, manufacture, etc. . . .' Each card contains a written description of a country.

One final English geographical pack worthy of mention appeared in the nineteenth century—'The New Geographical Cards' published by C. Hodges in London in 1827. Once again each suit was devoted to a single continent. Hearts = Europe, spades = America, diamonds = Asia, and clubs = Africa. The pip values are arranged in conventional fashion, full-sized, superimposed on maps. The court cards depict some of the inhabitants of the continents, either in general or individually— George IV and George Washington are kings of hearts and spades respectively. Australia puts in an appearance as part of Asia, divided into the two parts of New Holland and New South Wales. A French version is also known.

Apart from geography, however, instructive cards were not over-numerous in the eighteenth century. There were a few examples of historical cards—a pack depicting the kings of England appeared in about 1770: it showed full-length por-traits of the kings of England from William I to George II— this was not sufficient to fill fifty-two cards, so, for good measure, some ancient Britons appeared on the 2–5 of hearts and the spade numerals carry simple school exercises. The value is shown by a miniature card in a top corner.

Generally speaking the trend was towards cards of diversion. The Proverbs, Pastime and Delightful cards of Lenthall's list were forerunners of many handsome and most interesting packs. *The Beggar's Opera*, published in London in c. 1728, is a rare and splendid pack: miniature standard cards show the value in the top left corner and the rest of each card is devoted to the music and lyrics of some part of the Opera. Two other musical packs, probably issued some fifty years afterwards, are devoted to dance music of the day. One gives music only, the other also gives the title of the dance. A fourth item worthy of note was a pack of songs, with similar format to the others, published about 1730. Each card contains the lyrics and music and has a title at the top; for example, 'Advice to Celia' on the 8 of spades, 'Bright Cloe' on the 7 of diamonds.

Aesop's Fables was another fine pack issued in London in 1759 illustrating a number of the fables and having the tale and moral, in rhyme, at the foot of each card. The title of the fable is given at the top and the value is indicated by a miniature standard card at the top left.

London Cries is another, self-explanatory pack. This appeared in 1795 and shows various vendors crying their wares, such as the lady on the 3 of clubs who cries 'Hot Cross Bunns, One a Penny two a penny, hot Cross Bunns'. There is a London view in the background of each one, and the value is indicated by a miniature standard card in the top left-hand corner. The cries issue forth from the crier's mouth in the form of a balloon.

A less attractively engraved pack appeared at the end of the century to elaborate upon the *Vices and Virtues* with the former allegorically portrayed on the black suits and the latter on the red. Values were shown by a single suit-mark at top left plus a roman numeral or the word King, Queen or Knave. The allegorical picture is shown in a circle under which is its name and description. Anger is on the 3 of clubs, Liberality on the 9 of hearts, etc.

Two other eighteenth-century instructive packs combine diversion with education. The first is T. Foubert's Alphabetical Pack of 1757: each card, except the kings, has in the centre a dice mark, the value being shown by a suit-mark and roman numeral in top left corner. Jacks are full-length figures of David Garrick in different roles. At the right are three forms of a letter of the alphabet—capital, lower case and italic. On several cards there are little exercises in English and French. Kings show bust portraits of sovereigns, with George II on the king of hearts. The second is a Natural History pack with a bird or animal depicted on each card with its name written above. Values are shown by miniature standard cards in top left corner. On the ace of spades the centre of the miniature card face is taken up by a punchbowl and a piece of lemon.

England clearly held pride of place as regards European engraved cards of the eighteenth century, but elsewhere a few isolated packs were made of exceptional quality. Usually their origins are apparent, such as the German-suited astronomical cards made at Nuremberg in 1719, and some Italian-made Biblical cards made by Visentini in 1748 with curious suit-marks and arrangement—the suits were hearts (lettered a to nn), yellow diamonds (O to Z), orange circles (A to NN), and lavender jars (o to z): they depict and describe Biblical scenes and were designed by Francesco Zuccarelli.

Switzerland produced two of her few eighteenth-century engraved packs in 1744, when Hauser of Geneva published the *Jeu d'Officiers*, a 52-card pack depicting soldiers in costume from various parts of Europe—Germans, Highlanders, Pandures, etc. A caption at the foot of each card is written out in French, German and Italian. The value is indicated by a single suit-mark at top left plus a roman numeral or word Roi, Dame or Valet. Some courts portray contemporary royalty. A second, redrawn, edition omitted these portraits and substituted further officers. This is known as the *Nouveau Jeu d'Officiers*.

Another notable pack which emerged from Germany was a Calligraphic Pack made by J. C. Albrecht in 1769, on which intricate figures based on cards from the Hauser packs were designed entirely from the ingenious use of calligraphic charac-teristics. Examples of different scripts are also included on the cards. They are, in their execution, certainly quite unlike any other pack I have ever seen. The value is shown by a single suit-mark plus roman numeral.

Such was the variety of illustration on eighteenth-century cards. Before moving on to the new influences which seem directly to have stemmed from the French Revolution, I should perhaps mention Rowley's cards. These were issued in London in about 1785 and were an effort to introduce a new suit-system into England. The suits were cups, pikes, facetted diamonds and trefoils (shaped rather differently from the normal club suit). The reigning monarchs of England, France, Russia and Prussia were portrayed on the courts, with soldiers as knaves. The pip values were arranged in standard fashion. The idea never became popular.

CHAPTER VIII

From Revolutionary France to the Present Day

I HAVE already mentioned on page 58 the effect of the French Revolution upon French cards. The first noticeable trend, once peace was temporarily restored in Europe, was that with non-standard cards, apart from transformations which are discussed below, the practice of employing a whole pack to elaborate a theme ceased and in future a vast majority of messages on non-standard cards were contained on the court cards and aces only, and also on the trump cards of French-suited tarots.

Transformation cards are a rather different case. The exact date of their origin is unknown but it must have been within a few years of 1800 and not far from the Austro-German border. There was a considerable fashion for them throughout the nineteenth century, and a great deal of ingenuity was expended upon their design. They are certainly great fun to study; their aim is to 'transform' an ordinary pip card into a picture by means of incorporating the pips in their standard positions in a larger overall design (see plate V). Lazy card-makers were not above pirating many of the designs and often packs are difficult to identify without the presence of a maker's name on the cards.

Some of the first and some of the most celebrated of this type of card were in a series of packs made by Cotta, a bookseller of Tubinga, Württemberg, between 1805 and 1811. They were issued at yearly intervals (except 1809). Each year the court cards indicated some different theme and the actual transformation cards, the pip cards, were also newly designed. It is thought that the issues of 1805, 1806, 1808 and 1811 were all drawn by the same person, and the others by two different people; that of 1810 by Osiander who also designed and issued a pack of his own shortly after the Cotta series ceased. I have added a short description of this at the end of the Cotta list.

1st issue 1805: Courts depict characters from Schiller's *Jeanne D'Arc*.

2nd issue 1806: Courts depict Ulysses and various other classical figures. This issue was widely pirated.

3rd issue 1807: Schiller's *Wallenstein* characters on courts. (See plate V.)

4th issue 1808: Courts show figures in Arabian costume.

5th issue 1810: Mythological and comical characters on courts.

6th issue 1811: The courts depict various knightly orders.

Osiander's cards. These have rather small suit-marks and the courts portray the leaders of the allied armies (Wellington, Blücher, etc.) as kings; symbolic figures of England, Prussia, Austria and Russia as queens, and the countries' soldiers as jacks. This must have been one of the first of several examples of the allied leaders appearing on court cards of packs but is I think probably the only transformation pack with such characteristics.

An early and accurate copy of the second Cotta issue was made by Terquem and May of Metz in about 1830 and a less successful piracy was committed by Olivatte in England in 1828. The maker's name in all instances is to be found on the ace of clubs.

Some English packs were among the most interesting and amusing of early transformation cards. They copied each other's designs shamelessly and it is extremely difficult to identify exactly the various packs from single or only a few cards.

S. and T. Fuller 'at the Temple of Fancy, Rathbone Place, London' issued a pack in 1811 entitled *Transformation of cards Metastasis*. A similar pack was issued round about the same time under the same title, but the court cards are different and the pip cards have either different captions or relettered captions or, in some instances, are of quite different design: the artist's name appears on several of the cards and for this reason, without knowing the publisher's name I am calling these I. L. S. Cowell's transformations.

The court cards of the Fuller pack are mainly grotesque figures in the caricature style of the day and probably lampoon contemporary personalities. The king of hearts 'I think this attitude will suit me' may be Beau Brummel, the king of spades is a French marshal with a finger on a map of Spain which lies on a table the legs of which are being sawn in half by a small cherub underneath. The jack of hearts is a butcher holding up a heart and the jack of spades is a gravedigger.

The courts on the Cowell pack are nicely engraved standard figures with animal faces, and a border of miniature playing cards. The queen of spades, for example, is a cat, the jack of clubs a ram.

The pip cards are less easy to separate although the fine copperplate script in which the captions of Fuller's pack are drawn is noticeably different from the italic of the Cowell pack (see Plate V).

Many of the captions are great fun. One which might well shame the inventor of a modern advertising campaign shows a hostess putting a large dish before her guest and merely utters the three Greek letters 'Eta beta pi' (Fuller's 8 of diamonds). Another Fuller card, the 6 of hearts shows a sad sequence of events:

'Doctor McGill
Is Rather ill
And Physic tries
At length he will
Take his own pill
And then he dies'

Here are some examples of cards with the same design and different captions:

		Fuller	*Cowell*
ace of diamonds	a gay little figure sits on a mush-room strumming a lute	Robin Goodfellow	Fairies Revel
ace of spades	a chimpanzee beats a drum	Chimpanzee, in the Pantomime of Perouse, Covent Garden Theatre	In the Pantomime of Perouse

Yet another pack of extremely similar cards were issued at about the same time, one by S. W. Fores of Piccadilly in 1808. The courts are once again unlike any others. The king of hearts is a seated king to whom Cupid presents a basket of hearts: the queen is seated in a chariot and the jack is a cupid flying a heart. Again the jack of spades is a gravedigger but in this pack displays a skull. From the cards from this pack which I have in my collection, the design appears much more fussy in style than in the two previously mentioned, and there are very few captions (see plate V).

There is evidence of a fourth pack of the period with designs identical in style with the Fuller pack and having designs known in both the Fuller and Cowell versions. This may simply have been a second edition or variation of the original Fuller pack. I have only seen a few of such cards and have so far been unable to trace a complete pack.

Apart from the piracy of a Cotta pack by Olivatte in 1828, the vogue for transformation cards seemed to lapse in England until the 1850s. The one exception was the production in Ackermann's *Repository* in 1819, in the form of thirteen sheets showing four cards each, of a pack originally produced in Vienna by Müller, and known as *Beatrice* or *The Fracas*. It is printed in stipple and does not display much regard for the strict rules of design of transformation cards—if the pips do not fit in with the design, they are placed therein just the same. The subjects of the pip cards are rather exotic, with many processions, high priests and sepulchral scenes, the courts depicting historical figures, often of warlike character (they are known both with plain background and with decorative background): the kings are a Roman general (hearts), a crowned king (spades), a Turkish monarch (diamonds) and Alexander the Great (clubs). Of the latter card the *Repository* comments: 'This monarch will perhaps remind our readers of a justly celebrated modern actor when engaged in personifying a hero of Greece or Rome, as a similar attitude is well and often chosen by him; the similarity of action is accidental, but it is striking...'

The pack had a further publication by C. Bartlett in New York in 1833.

Müller of Vienna had previously issued two similar packs, with fanciful and theatrical courts, but neither seem to have achieved the popularity or widespread distribution of *The Fracas*.

In the new France two transformation packs with the same pip cards were issued in 1819: the courts of one showing satirical interpretations of reactionary newspapers of the time (the courts are named—Constitutionnel, Minerve, Figaro, Moniteur, Lettres Normandes, Don-Quichotte, Quotidienne, etc.) and theatres of the period on the other (Vaudeville, Gymnase, Cirque Olympique, Opéra, Opéra Buffa, Variétés, etc.). Some of the pip cards might be deemed slightly risqué, depending as they do on the rear human anatomy for illustrating the heart and spade suits. The captions are in French.

Another early French pack worthy of mention is that designed by Baron d'Athalin in the reign of Louis Philippe. The courts are readily identifiable as being finely drawn representations of the standard names given to French courts (i.e. the kings are Charles, David, Alexander and Caesar). The pip cards display a great feeling for movement.

Another rather later pack (I have so far only been able to trace it in sheet form) was issued simultaneously in England, Vienna, Munich and America in about 1850. Unless whole sheets of the cards are procured, it is not always easy to tell the editions apart, but if the sheets are obtained, little verses at the top, and possibly the publishers' names at the bottom, are usually evident (one suit occupies each page or sheet). They are known with some German captions, with some English captions and without any captions. Cards of the diamonds suit have the monogram JB on the bottom right corner. The king of hearts shows a Bacchus figure astride a barrel. Many of the pip cards have designs also found in the next series of packs to be described. These packs, clearly copied from one another, emerged at about the same time, taking advantage of the new printing process of chromolithography. It is not always easy to tell which edition is which although it is thought editions were printed in Darmstadt, Leipzig, and Paris. B. P. Grimaud of Paris printed his name on the jack of hearts and used a larger format than the other makers. Grimaud also used a greater number of original designs—the Darmstadt and Leipzig cards took a number of the cards described above and added the new chromolithographed courts (this also happened in America)· These courts, which differ slightly from pack to pack, are as follows for the Grimaud pack:

King of hearts: Cupid figure.
Queen of hearts: Ballet dancer.
Jack of hearts: Servant delivering a letter.
King of spades: A Red Indian chief.
Queen of spades: Joan of Arc.
Jack of spades: A beadle. (My Darmstadt pack shows the peasant with a scythe found on the jack of clubs.)
King of diamonds: A medieval king. (The Darmstadt pack and, I understand, the Leipzig pack both show an allegorical American king with an eagle and shield bearing stars and stripes.)
Queen of diamonds: Market woman. (This design appears on the queen of clubs in the Darmstadt pack and the Swiss peasant girl on the queen of diamonds.)
Jack of diamonds: A servant sweeping. (A huntsman with a slaughtered stag on the Darmstadt pack.)

King of clubs: A tippling Boniface on a donkey.

Queen of clubs: Swiss peasant girl. (See queen of diamonds.)

Jack of clubs: Peasant with a scythe. (A beadle on the Darmstadt pack.)

The Darmstadt pack was made by Fromme und Bunte as late as 1870. Generally speaking the series is referred to as the Joan of Arc transformation pack but should not be confused with the much rarer early Cotta issue.

Whatever the problems of copyright, piracy and general rivalry, by the 1870s the final wave of transformation cards seems to have broken in calmer seas and become less difficult to differentiate. Reynolds and Sons in England brought out a pack with standard double-ended court cards and transformation pip cards with captions mostly punning on some form of card or play ('Ready to Deal', 'Two for a Pair', 'Playing for Love', 'Taking up a Card', etc.). At about the same time a pack was issued in Manchester with charming but rather amateurish drawings and non-standard court cards (the spade courts are all occupied with the garden, hearts with the preparation and theft of tarts, diamonds with the king counting his money and his wife eating honey, and clubs with those who use such instruments as weapons). This pack was issued at one time by Maclure, Macdonald and Macgregor and at another by John Galloway, both of Manchester.

In 1876 William Makepeace Thackeray designed twenty-one transformation cards which appear in the first edition of his *The Orphan of Pimlico*. This work will provide the collector with a unique and inexpensive example of a celebrated author and artist turning his hand to card design.

In France the Second Empire witnessed the appearance of a pack containing very finely delineated pip transformations with such eccentricities as an insect orchestra on the 4 of clubs, and circus jugglers on the 10 of clubs. The king of clubs is a smartly dressed contemporary man-about-town and the jack of diamonds is the inevitable servant delivering a letter.

In 1873 a further, artistically less refined pack appeared in

Paris with animals on the court cards. These are named *Dame*, *Valet*, *Roi*, so are not to be confused with the Cowell pack.

The last examples of transformations that I know of come from the United States. The *Harlequin* transformation pack, designed by Carryl, was issued first in full-size format by Tiffany and Co. and then in a cigarette card format by Kinney Tobacco Co. The pip cards are extremely colourful and lively and cover such subjects as 'Vassar taking the air', 'A Mississippi Minuet', 'Finnigan's Wake' and so forth. The court cards are caricatures of single-figure standard courts and the jacks are symbolic figures of the U.S.A., Germany, France and England.

However, these cards, although perhaps the most celebrated of the American transformations, were not the first; for the *Eclipse Comic Playing Cards* were made three years earlier by Lowerre. Then followed, in the 1880s, several advertising transformation packs, such as that made by Dougherty for Murphy's Varnish, and another famous pack of the period was made by the U.S. Playing Card Co. of Cincinnati—*Hustling Joe Playing Cards*.

But the era of transformations had virtually drawn to a close. Cardmakers presumably balked at the expense of producing or commissioning fifty-two separate designs on a single pack of cards. Nevertheless there is no reason why the nineteenth-century vogue for copying or creating by hand by any individual cannot be continued. I have several examples of such cards, varying greatly in quality, but when faced with the problem myself I rarely get past the simplest designs for the low numerals on the diamond suit.

A second vogue evident in European (but not English) cards was the attention accorded to the relatively newly introduced French-suited tarot pack.

It has already been noted that this type of card was introduced to the central part of Europe (the Empire, south Germany and the Low Countries) in the second half of the eighteenth century. The more or less standard packs settled down into having animals, natural history, or rural scenes on their trump cards fairly quickly. But right from the start the novelty or non-standard trump cards achieved popularity. There is no necessity to give long descriptions of these cards as most packs have maker's name and address and a tax stamp indicating the date somewhere in the pack. The earliest examples clearly existed up to forty or fifty years prior to 1800 but the heyday of the fashion was not in full swing until the nineteenth century.

One of the earliest packs was by Albrecht of Innsbruck, depicting battle scenes. By 1770 the animal tarots were known in Germany and Belgium (they never seemed to catch on in Austria) and within a decade a musical pack (depicting both musicians and music) appeared in Leipzig. At about the same time a cardmaker in Dresden published a wood-block pack depicting a variety of soldiers from Central Europe. A little later A. B. Göbl of Munich produced the celebrated and handsome *Wedding Feast* pack. So that by 1800 the style of card was well established.

In the nineteenth century the principal publishers of these cards were Austrians, although Budapest, Prague, Germany, Brussels, Schaffhausen and Paris also had their own makers of such cards. But the majority of the most elegant and interesting designs came from the houses of Müller, J. G. or Max Uffenheimer, Piatnik, Estel, Hofman, Titze & Schinkay and Josef Glanz, all of Vienna.

Mythological and also local contemporary scenes were popular subjects, as well as *chinoiserie*, the rage for which pervaded Western Europe. Up till 1848 all cards had straightforward themes and presentations, with nothing to tax the conservative conscience of the day. The Uffenheimers produced such packs as *Scott's Novels* and *Viennese views*, Mayer & Wilner in Pesth produced a rebus tarot with pictured word problems (see plate VI), Müller issued a 'Turkish' tarot and Koller another pack of Viennese views. Many such packs enjoyed a life and sale lasting ten or twenty years—as differently dated tax stamps on different copies of the same pack will testify.

By 1848 several of these cardmakers had dropped out, leaving Piatnik and Glanz as principal makers of these cards.

The political upheavals of that year introduced, as the Revolution in France had done, a new element of satire in the design of some cards. A rare pack satirizing the state issued by Glanz round about this time was strongly disapproved of by the authorities (see plate VI). A delightful pack issued by Glanz was a hunting tarot depicting on several trumps occasions when the hunter became more or less hunted.

Another popular Glanz pack was a war tarot issued in several editions (distinguishable by the growth of beard on the face of Franz Josef I on trump no. II, and also the different borders to the design) showing scenes from various wars, it would appear, including that against Denmark.

Other subjects dealt with by the many cardmakers included Mardi Gras costumes, flowers, leisure occupations, authors, street cries, burlesque, shadow portraits and so on. In 1906, for the purposes of raising funds for charity, a pack with toy-like figures appeared and this was one of the last of a flood of such cards. Piatnik issued a war tarot in about 1917 which went so far as to show a U-boat in New York Harbour but since that time standard designs have been more or less the order of the day in all tarot-producing countries.

Fortune-telling cards also held the interest of many in the nineteenth century. Here again, the beginning of the fashion lay in the second half of the eighteenth century although most fortune-telling cards were issued in the nineteenth. An eighteenth-century barber named Alliette devised a pack based on a 78-card Italian-suited tarot pack and invested each card, frantically redesigned, with some grave significance. He reversed his name and called himself Etteilla and a number of packs have appeared right up to the present bearing this mystical name. The trump cards are in fact named which is sometimes the only way of appreciating their relationship with the conventional tarot pack. The suit-marks are not in their usual positions, often being scattered all over the card. Other fortune-telling tarot packs have been issued, notably one in England designed by Pamela Coleman-Smith some time about 1916 which was also copied in Ireland and the U.S.A.; a version of the latter edition is still on sale today. To my mind, these have over-romanticized and over-dogmatic presentations of the cards: the high-priest and high-priestess take over from the Pope and Popess, and the money suit is called the pentacles suit. The clubs are called batons. Another little tarot pack with many similar characteristics was produced in bright reds and yellows in Dundee in the 1920s or 1930s, and since the last war the Insight Institute has produced a tarot pack in England which draws on the Coleman-Smith pack, *minchiate* packs, and standard Italian tarot packs for its designs. A pack in France, *Les Arcanes du Destin*, has, curiously enough, the design of the standard Piedmontese double-headed tarot pack but names the courts in some sort of dog Latin. Modiano of Trieste has also issued a pack with romantic delineations of the trump cards and the conventional pip cards.

The fashion of fortune-telling may have begun in the sixteenth century, but it seems highly likely that with very few exceptions (such as Lenthall's cards), cartomancy was practised with conventional standard cards until the coming of Etteilla. France undoubtedly issued most fortune-telling cards, and these are usually identifiable by the language of the inscriptions and the presence of a miniature standard card in the design. Germany did not at first seem to have taken the craze very seriously and merely produced some rather elegantly engraved little cards with suitably ambiguous little comments. Then, in the second half of the nineteenth century, a form of fortune-telling card was evolved which might now almost be called standard in its own right, as it is still issued in many countries. The pack is sometimes called the Lenormand fortune-telling pack (not to be confused with Mlle Lenormand's large complex pack showing mythological figures, constellations, and other significant signs) and consists of only thirty-six cards, usually numbered. A miniature conventional card shows the playing card value at the top centre and the rest of the card is devoted to some realistic scene or incident. B. Dondorf of Frankfurt made a lot of these cards; they have been made in England and two versions (one large, one small) were issued as cigarette cards between the wars: I also have a nineteenth century Italian version made in Milan and I am sure they have been made in or at least imported into most other card-playing countries.

Most fortune-telling cards are easy to identify. Some are boring in their intense seriousness; others with the lighter touch achieve more distinction.

I have noted in passing that the personalities engaged in fighting Napoleon appear on the courts of the Osiander transformation cards. They also appeared on a number of other packs and are examples of a fashion for using contemporaries as subjects for court cards although the practice was not completely unknown before. Many interesting portraits have appeared on cards since, often of royalty, sometimes of politicians. The crowned heads of Europe appeared on the courts of a beautifully engraved and hand-coloured pack which was one of a series issued in Paris in the 1850s (see plate VII). Politicians were caricatured in two packs of *Deakin's Political Playing Cards* in England in the 1880s; Dondorf and Wüst, both of Frankfurt, issued many packs for export with recognizable portraits of royalty or other notables; Germany issued packs with both German and French suits depicting the Royal Family and the Generals during the First World War; and after the Second World War two packs were issued, one in Belgium, one in France, of the Allied leaders. There are many similar packs.

Wüst and Dondorf also issued packs with near-conventional but non-standard or straightforward portrait courts and with 'scenic' aces depicting geographical or historical scenes ranging from views of Batavia to the Battle of Sebastopol. And Dutch, Belgian, Austrian and French makers made similar packs. These are far too numerous to list but it should be noted that from them developed the first type of souvenir card. These coincided with the increased fashion for touring in the 1860s. One of the first of these packs was made at about that time by Wüst of Frankfurt for export to Switzerland: it showed Swiss views on the aces and the local costumes of the Cantons on the courts.

There have since been many such packs from various parts of Europe.

The success of such packs must have inevitably led to the straightforward photographic souvenir pack, the first of which probably appeared in the 1890s. These packs consisted of fifty-two views, usually of a set area, and the values of the cards are simply indicated by a suit-mark and numeral or letter in the corners. Early packs of these cards are most interesting and deal with such subjects as *The Yukon Pass*, *Ocean to Ocean* (a Canadian pack) and, one out-of-bounds pack, *The Boxer Rebellion*. Later ones deal with every possible area—Ireland, Germany, Spain, London, Scotland, East Africa, South Africa, New Zealand and so on, until finally Pan American covered the whole world in an advertising pack. America in particular has issued a great number of these packs and a comprehensive picture album of the U.S.A. could be compiled from a collection of such cards. Another category widely illustrated and commemorated on such cards are World Fairs and Exhibitions.

Mention of Pan American leads to the subject of advertising cards in general. The idea of Mr Tuttle's cards advertising his wares in Lenthall's list did not come to fruition until about 175 years later in the United States. The transformation packs already mentioned must have been among the first of such cards but it is in the twentieth century that the principal examples of such cards are to be found. By and large, expense in producing a specially designed pack has led to companies and corporations merely stamping some advertising copy or design on the backs of standard cards, but those who persevered in issuing whole new packs have provided some interesting collectors' items: Roget et Galler, the Schering Corporation, Hoover, Ostend/Dover Shipping Line, *Time Magazine*, and K.L.G. are a few of the famous firms who have published such packs.

Of course there are many non-standard packs which do not fall into any of the above categories. These might loosely be termed as 'artistic' or 'novel'. From time to time, companies issue limited editions of such cards which have no other object than to be visually attractive. A modern French firm, Philibert, for example, published several packs in the 1950s falling into the 'artistic' category; one is called *Florentin* and the courts depict Renaissance figures; another is called *Can-Can* and courts and four extra aces depict scenes easily imagined. Another recent French pack shows cartoon characters (the Little King, Dagwood, Pop-eye, etc.) on the courts. In England Waddington's have issued a pack entitled the *Four Elements*, the courts of each suit being devoted to one of the elements; and De La Rue celebrated their 125th anniversary by issuing a pack elaborately designed by Picart Le Doux. The novelty classification also covers the vast quantity of packs published which are simply collections of fifty-two pin-up pictures; these vary greatly in quality as may be imagined. Possibly an earlier version of these ubiquitous cards was known in France in the middle of the last century when daring semi-pornographic 'transparent' cards were made—apparently normal cards which when held up to the light revealed a hidden design. Being much sought after by collectors of pornography they tend to fetch extremely high prices!

Cigarette and candy cards (i.e. one given away with each packet) have appeared from time to time ever since the 1890s and should presumably be categorized somewhere between novel and advertising. Early English examples of this type of card were usually in the form of an attractive design with miniature standard cards in the top corners: *Indian Beauties* was one such pack, *Exotic Birds* another, and music hall heroines appear on another. More recently the Dandy Chewing Gum Co. issued a pack of pin-ups. Another depicted units of the British Army. In Belgium and Holland several candy sets have appeared, including those depicting film stars, vintage or modern cars, footballers and the like. Before World War II Liebeg's issued a pack of children's miniature fortune-telling cards (with the same methods of distribution, in connection with one of their products): collectors of complete packs were then entitled to participate in a draw for prizes. In modern cards of this kind the value is simply shown by a suit-mark and number or letter.

Indeed it is almost safe to say that with modern non-standard cards anything may turn up; from a study of Icelandic mythology to a souvenir of a *Gala de Publicité*; from a modern version of the original Paris pattern to scenic aces showing views of the Isle of Man: all are worth the collector's consideration.

CHAPTER IX

The New World

WHERE the early explorers went, playing cards went too. Spanish cards were introduced to much of South America, Mexico and southern parts of what are now the United States; Portuguese cards went to Brazil, English cards appeared in New England, the West Indies and parts of Canada—where at first French cards (Paris pattern) were also imported for the French population. Nowadays the U.S.A. and Canada use standard English cards almost exclusively and the Spanish-suited cards (as well as the standard English) are only found in Mexico and points south. In South America, although they make their own cards, there has been little development of design and the Spanish-suited cards from that part of the world have little individual interest.

Canada has the distinction of having at one time used playing cards as money. In 1685 the authorities were desperately short of money with which to pay troops who were threatening to mutiny, and so all playing cards were confiscated and reissued as paper money. This practice continued for nearly seventy-five years—the cards were used whole, in halves or in quarters and were signed by the governor who also wrote on them the proposed value. In spite of their long life these cards are extremely rare and much sought after.

On the whole, Canada imported her cards, first from France and England, then England, then the U.S.A., and the history of their design is indistinguishable from these countries; indeed I have never been able to find really old Canadian cards. Canada was, nevertheless, early on the scene with the vogue for souvenir cards at the end of the nineteenth century although many of the early products of this kind of pack were specially made in England and imported.

The United States has had a more interesting history of card production than the rest of North and South America. Early Spanish adventurers introduced their cards to the South-West and soon the local Indians were enjoying the mysteries of card playing. Such packs were made from improvised materials, often leather, and even in this century such cards have been found in use among the Indians of the South-West, although their neighbours with European origins have in the main long ceased to use them.

While the States were colonies of European countries, with very few possible exceptions printed cards were imported from the mother country. Many English cards issued in the eighteenth century are known with the word EXPORTATION at the foot of their ace of spades and doubtless many of these found their way to America. This trade must have been stopped almost entirely after the War of Independence, and from that time onwards the cardmakers of the United States did flourishing business.

The old English standard pattern was retained although the old taxed English ace of spades was replaced by a variety of designs incorporating the American eagle and the maker's name. A few artistically engraved non-standard packs were made in the early part of the nineteenth century, notably by Jazaniah Ford of Milton, Massachusetts (probably the first official cardmaker in the States) and J. Y. Humphreys of Philadelphia, both in the delicate style of Austrian cards of the period.

But original design was the exception rather than the rule right up to the Civil War. By this time Samuel Hart of Philadelphia (1849–71) and Andrew Dougherty of New York were the main producers of cards and the latter brought out a pack called *Army and Navy Cards* with fanciful suits—drummer boys, zouaves, monitors, and Merrimac—in 1865. These were not, however, the first Civil War cards—these were probably the *Union Playing Cards* made by the American Card Company of

New York in 1862: they also had fancy suits—flags, stars, shields and eagles. For the Confederacy, Goodall of London made a pack but this had standard faces with a Confederate flag motif on the back. Another Northern pack was made by M. Nelson of New York in 1863 which depicted Union generals.

After the Civil War, U.S. cardmakers seem to have engaged in as feverish an activity as any of their European contemporaries and often the same type of card was the result. The transformations emerged, there were caricature cards, round cards were made by the Globe Card Company of Boston in 1874, fortune-telling cards abounded, pin-ups made a modest appearance, the Columbian Exposition of 1893 was commemorated on cards, and the tobacco industry showed the way to advertising on cigarette cards.

In the twentieth century the number of cardmakers had, as elsewhere, shrunk to a few firms dominating the industry. Still, in the 1960s there has been a noticeable increase in the publication of artistic or novelty packs by smaller individual firms. There is also apparent a degree of specialization—Brown and Bigelow of St Paul, Minnesota, for example, publish a large variety of souvenir packs; another company in St Louis, Missouri, issues packs with comic themes. The United States Playing Card Company of Cincinnati (which owns a splendid collection of European and American playing cards) is the natural descendant of many earlier makers of standard (and some other) cards, who gradually absorbed one another.

Apart from the variations of design of the fronts of cards, the U.S. is a happy hunting-ground for the collectors of card backs, aces of spades (so much more diverse in design than the English) and decorative jokers. Every possible theme has been represented on the backs of cards and many collectors specialize in single subjects, such as railroad or steamship advertising, royalty, museum subjects, bird-life, etc. The choice of theme is clearly a matter for the individual collector, so all I would point out is that there is a great deal of scope for trading with other collectors in the United States, both for single cards and complete packs.

CHAPTER X

Asia

THIS short chapter may well be a matter of first things coming last. Mr William Chatto in his *Facts and Speculations on the Origin and History of Playing Cards* makes quite a good case for cards originating in the East and it is also claimed elsewhere that Chinese cards were known before A.D. 1000.

Whatever the origins, the collecting of Asiatic playing cards tends to be hard on any collector without a knowledge of Asiatic languages, and I can only offer aids to the identification of certain of the principal forms of packs. India provides the only really obviously pictorial as well as serial suit-system; most Asiatic cards, having no suit sequences, should probably not be classed as playing cards at all: however, most collectors accept these items so I will do my best to describe them.

The most usual form of Persian pack is the *Asnas* set which basically comprises five designs each repeated four times; each design being associated with its own coloured background. The colours are more constant in *Asnas* packs than the designs thereon but roughly speaking they are intended always to represent the same identity; these are:

Black	*As*	Lion	Or other fierce animal: I have a pack in which a knight is killing a dragon on the black colour cards
Green	*Padishah*	King	A mounted or enthroned king
Yellow	*Bibi*	Queen	A female figure, not necessarily regal
Red	*Lakkat* or *Couli*	Dancer	A dancer, or sometimes a huntsman

| Gold | *Sarbaz* | Soldier | On my packs this figure has more the appearance of a hunter |

Persian cards of this type are small (about 2 in. x 1¼ in.) and made of paper which has been stiffened by lacquer; they are handpainted. I cannot discover whether these cards are still in use although they certainly were at the beginning of the century: the basic form of the pack can be multiplied or added to depending on the number of players the set is intended for.

Persian cards are rectangular in shape: 99 per cent of Indian cards are circular with a diameter ranging from about one inch to about four inches. The remaining 1 per cent are mostly very old cards (eighteenth century) which can still be distinguished from Persian by the suit-system, although the method of production (lacquered paper, or ivory for luxury packs) is the same. All traditional Indian cards are hand-made.

The two packs most often to come the way of the collector are the eight-suit and ten-suit packs known as *Gandjifah* (this word also means 'playing cards' in a general sense) and *Dasavatara* respectively. Each has suits of twelve cards comprising two courts, king (*Mir*) and vizier (*Pradhan*) and ten pip cards, 1–10. In the *Gandjifah* pack the suits are said to represent the various aspects of life in the court of an Indian prince (including the basic ingredients of night and day) and there are four superior suits and four inferior suits which are as follows:

Superior suits	*Taj*	Crown
	Soofed	Originally derived from the word for a silver coin, the suit symbol is a moon
	Shumsher	A sabre
	Gholam	A slave
Inferior suits	*Chung*	A harp
	Soorkh	A red or gold coin originally, this soon became figured as the sun
	Burat	A diploma or missive
	Quimash	Merchandise which usually looks rather like a paper parcel

The viziers are all shown as mounted on horses except those of slaves (on a bullock), harps (a camel) and sun (a tiger). The suits vary slightly from pack to pack but are constant enough for identification. Very old packs show cards on the same coloured background throughout but later cards usually vary colours from suit to suit: here again the system is not entirely consistent but almost invariably the moon suit has a black background, sabres a red one and the sun a green. These cards are rarely more than 2 inches in diameter.

The second pack, the *Dasavatara*, has ten suits of twelve cards, each representing one of the ten incarnations or avatars of Vishnu. As with the other pack the symbolism by which a suit is depicted varies, as does the style of execution. In general *Dasavatara* cards are more detailed and elaborate in design than the *Gandjifah*. The cards are anything up to four or five inches in diameter. The suits are:

1.	*Matsyavatara*	The fish
2.	*Kourmavatara*	The tortoise
3.	*Varahavatara*	The wild boar
4.	*Narasinhavatara*	The lion
5.	*Vamanavatara*	The Brahmin dwarf (sometimes a dwarf, sometimes a water vase suit)
6.	*Parasou-Rama*	The axe
7.	*Rama-Ichandra*	The bow and arrow (sometimes the suit is a bow and arrow, sometimes monkeys)
8.	*Krishna*	The thunderbolt (this is either represented by a quoit-shaped thunderbolt or by cows)
9.	*Buddha*	The conch (the kingly umbrella sometimes replaces the conchshell)
10.	*Calki-avatara*	The horse

I have not attempted a direct translation of the avatars but have only indicated the symbols used to portray them.

Some Indian packs are fantastic in their complexity; I have part of a *Chamundeshwari* pack (from south India) which, if complete, has sixteen suits, each representing a god or mytho-logical figure and each having eighteen cards comprising six courts (the suit-figure enthroned, in a carriage, in a palanquin, on an elephant, on a horse, on a palace roof) and twelve pip cards bearing the signs of the Zodiac. In addition there are twenty-five *Shakti* or trump cards and seven wild cards—three hundred and twenty cards in all! There are several other equally complex packs from the same region.

Orissa is another area rich in types of cards. One is the twelve-suit *Ramayana* pack in which the suits are represented by background colours rather than the figures shown thereon. These colours are white, black, bright blue, dark blue, pale brown, dark brown, light red, dark red, pale yellow, lemon yellow, green and mauve. There are ten pip cards and two courts.

The richness of the Indian card-playing scene is undoubtedly due to the fact that each pack is unique, being hand-made, and the variety of design for the same type of pack is infinite. The luxury packs, often on ivory with a mass of delicate golden filigree design, can hardly be reconciled with a hastily put together pack of lacquered paper with the merest formality of an effort to represent the traditional suit-marks: slaves become simple blobs on top of straight lines, several other suits (moon, sun, diploma) just smears, and suits are only distinguish-able by background colouring. There is a very gradual degree of artistic quality between these two types. The vast difference in appearance between the luxury and most plebeian type of pack is shown by comparing the two cards of the same value on plate VIII.

Probably the finest accumulation of Indian cards is to be found in the Bielefeld Playing Card Company's Museum in Germany. So far as I know the most useful reference work on the subject is *Charta Lusoria* by the late Dr. Eberhard Pinder (see bibliography).

The Portuguese explorers and adventurers mentioned on a previous page did not call a halt in India. The dragon aces of their Spanish-suited cards have been traced at various stages in several parts of the Far East, from India itself to Japan, where the pack has been absorbed and adapted for local gambling purposes under the title of *Hozuki* or *The Winter Cherry*. The suit-marks are by now corrupted and are barely recognizable as the original cups, swords, money and clubs but with a little patience a pack can be made out as having four suits of twelve cards each. Apart from the modern bridge pack of the West and a curious union between the bridge pack and a national Japanese game, *Hana Garuta* or *The Flower Game*, Japanese cards do not have suits and should therefore be categorized as card games rather than playing cards.

The Flower Game is undoubtedly the most popular and contains forty-eight cards. These depict, in twelve sets of four cards, the flowers which reach their best in each month of the year: these are the Pine, Plum, Cherry, Wistaria, Iris, Peony, Lespedeza, the Moon, Chrysanthemum, Maple, then two sets representing Rain and *Pawlonia Imperialis* which forms the crest of the Emperor. For a number of years now versions of this pack have also been made with miniature standard English cards added to make up the full 52-card standard pack.

A majority of Japanese games seems to consist of one hundred or two hundred, or multiples of a hundred, cards which are divided into two sets which have to be matched one with another. Perhaps the most celebrated example of this is *Uta Garuta* or *The Song Game of the Hundred Poets of Japan*: this is a set of two hundred cards, a hundred of which bear portraits of famous poets, the other hundred bearing an example of each one's work: these have to be recognized and matched. Other such games are *Genji Garuta* in which the beginning and ending of poems referring to a celebrated romance of the tenth century *Genji Monogatari* have to be matched; *I-ro-ha Garuta*, or *The Alphabet Game*, in which the beginnings of songs (each beginning with a different syllable from the Japanese syllabary) are matched with their endings; *Jiyo Garuta* in which the two halves of classical quotations are matched; *Kokinshiu*, a 600-card pack in which the halves of ancient poems are matched; *Meisho Garuta*, *The Famous Views Game* in which poems and the places they describe are matched; *No-no Garuta* (*the Game of the Ancient Plays*) in which both series of fifty cards are illustrated alike but the captions vary (this pack is at least three hundred years old). Examples of these cards are to be found in the Phillips Collection at the Guildhall in London, and I must acknowledge my debt to the catalogue of the collection for the above list of games.

Japan today has entered the Western souvenir-type of card market. Recent productions include packs of Japanese pin-ups (illustrated in Japanese traditional style and by far the most attractive of this category of card), fifty-two cocktails, fifty-two types of gun and so on. This activity could hardly be classed as a national development in card history but is merely another example of the waves of fashion which sweep the whole card-making world regardless of individual traditions.

I have left the cards of China until almost last, since this is a big and daunting subject.

Although there appear to be only four different types of card originating in China, each type has innumerable offshoots and varieties. From lack of space as well as ignorance I do not intend to try a comprehensive survey of all Chinese cards, so the following can only be considered a basic springboard for further investigation.

Type 1. Cards derived from dice or dominoes. The basis of such packs is the series of twenty-one values obtainable from throwing dice; these are the twenty-one domino values. They are divided into two sections known as 'civilians' and 'military' and are as follows, in their order of value:

Civilians	*Local name*
6	
–	heaven
6	
1	
–	earth
1	
4	
–	man
4	

$\dfrac{1}{3}$ harmony *or* the geese

$\dfrac{5}{5}$ plums

$\dfrac{3}{3}$ long threes *or* door chain

$\dfrac{2}{2}$ the bench

$\dfrac{5}{6}$ tiger's head *or* the chopper

$\dfrac{4}{6}$ the screen

$\dfrac{1}{6}$ the water bucket

$\dfrac{1}{5}$ the hammer

Military

$\dfrac{4}{5}$ and $\dfrac{3}{6}$ nines

$\dfrac{2}{6}$ and $\dfrac{3}{5}$ eights

$\dfrac{3}{4}$ and $\dfrac{2}{5}$ sevens

$\dfrac{1}{4}$ and $\dfrac{2}{3}$ fives

2
— bighead six
4

1
— three chickens
2

1s and 4s are coloured red and the remainder black.

These twenty-one cards are usually repeated in different packs: some packs have the cards repeated six times, some four, others again have two sets of civilian cards and only one of military. Often the values are shown merely by domino spots, sometimes an illuminatory theme is introduced in the centre of the card and the value is indicated by miniature dominoes at top or bottom. Like all Chinese cards, these are long and narrow and as with other types of Chinese cards, several extra joker cards are sometimes included in the packs.

Type 2. Cards derived from Chessmen. This description sounds simple enough, but it is another matter to identify the various forms of Chinese chessmen which appear on these cards. The form of games played with the cards are also unrelated to the familiar chess figures, the object being to collect in one hand all versions of the same value contained in the pack. The cards consist of king, queen, bishop, rook, knight, cannon and pawn repeated several times in a variety of forms and in a varying number of colours (which might be called suits). The cannon is a piece known in Chinese chess although unfamiliar to Western players. Sample compilations of such packs are:

a: four each of the values, all in four different colours, plus five jokers known as the Five Blessings. Total, 117 cards.
b: four each of the values in two colours, no jokers. Total, 56 cards.

These cards are difficult to identify without a knowledge of Chinese.

Type 3. Cards derived from Coins. This type of card is found, with variations, over a vast area of China and the rest of south-east Asia, and the basic design differs in its execution as widely as the hand-made cards of India.

As in other Chinese packs, the basic cards are repeated a varying number of times, but generally speaking the characteristic cards number thirty, divided into three suits of nine cards plus three extra cards (more or less the equivalent of court cards). These suits are based on the Chinese coin called *cash* and are known as *cash*, strings of *cash* and myriads of *cash*. The *cash* suit cards, loosely speaking, depict single coins, and are known in some districts as the cakes suit. The strings of *cash* show piles of coins with strings protruding from the tops, and the myriads suit seems to be a series of portraits of wealthy gentlemen (some say celebrated gamblers) who presumably have in their possession myriads of *cash*. This suit indicates its values in a top panel by the characters for the suit name and the figure showing its worth. In addition each card has individual marks at top and bottom which relate to the numeral value and sometimes also to the suit. These 'squeezer' marks vary from region to region. The three extra cards are known as 'White-flower', 'Redflower' and 'Old Thousand', the maker's sign usually being stamped on these in red. Some packs are also known with extra jokers stamped in gold.

Sometimes, due to corruption of the original design, these cards are not easy to identify: the sort of variation of design which can be expected is shown by the cards illustrated on plate VIII.

Type 4. Cards derived from Words. These cards are marked according to the 'Happy Families' system: apparently arbitrarily chosen words or sayings are repeated, and the object of the game, as with many Chinese games, is to collect a certain number of the same card. The cards can be words from proverbs, numbers, and so on and have no individual value. Like other Chinese packs, this one also on occasion includes extra 'joker' cards such as the 'Five Blessings' (Posterity, Promotion, Long Life, Happiness and Wealth).

Further information about all these types of card can be found at the end of the O'Donoghue catalogue of the Schreiber collection of playing cards at the British Museum.

As a postscript to this chapter on Asiatic cards, Korea must be mentioned, although the subject of Korean playing cards has been skated over by those more erudite than I. Cards have been known in that country for many centuries and it is thought their origins closely coincide with those of Chinese cards: the form of the only packs that I have come across would tend to confirm this—cards are repeated several times and appear not to have any comparative value. A pack in my possession has sixty cards comprising nine sets of six identical cards plus an additional set of six cards which are all different. Korean cards on the whole are narrow (about half an inch) and much longer than Chinese (up to six or seven inches). I have illustrated one of these in plate VIII, but any further research on the subject should be carried out by individual collectors.

CHAPTER XI

Some Aids to Identity

I HOPE that the foregoing chapters give some idea of how to place packs of cards geographically although there are numerous packs to be found which defy positive identification (a high proportion of these emanate from Belgium whose cardmakers are notorious for their apparent desire to remain anonymous). Dating cards is another and more precarious matter; those wishing to sell playing cards without having any knowledge of the subject very often have an inflated idea of the age of cards merely because their wares seem unfamiliar.

Printing processes must afford some clues although these are not infallible. Apart from the sheer style of pre-nineteenth century engraved cards (bearing in mind that every card in a pack had its own illustration) the more common or garden method of wood-block printing plus hand stencil-colouring (used for most standard packs) survived until the mid-nineteenth century in France, England and Germany, and probably until the beginning of the twentieth century in Italy.

The nature of decorated backs to cards is not much more helpful: France and England retained plain backs well into the nineteenth century (with the inevitable exceptions) whereas the rest of Europe has had decorated backs to its cards in some form or another for centuries.

Cards with double-headed courts must also be assessed carefully. Generally speaking such cards were not used in England or the United States before the 1850s although there is in the British Museum an example of double-headed court cards which must have been made thirty to fifty years earlier (a double-headed version of Ludlow's Knights' cards). Other European countries, however, adopted the practice fairly generally, but by no means invariably, in the first quarter of the nineteenth century: some Italian packs (notably *tarocchino* packs) followed the practice even earlier.

Square corners on cards of reasonable quality usually indicate that they were made before 1890; this statement must be qualified by the reminder that avid card players are avid shufflers of cards, with the result that many cards which started with square corners quickly achieved round ones, a situation further complicated by enterprising merchants in Central Europe who were willing to clean and gild the (rounded) edges of used cards. A further guide here can be the frame-line to the design of a card; if this has square corners the card is likely to have had square corners to start with; if it is rounded, then the card belongs to the later period.

Indices were more late arrivals on the scene. These letters found in the corners of cards indicate the value of the cards in a manner which enables the player to identify them without fanning out his hand so that the whole of every card is visible: as far as I can make out, American card manufacturers may have evolved this idea in the 1870s. In Europe the practice would seem to have been adopted fairly widely by the 1890s. Different countries were apt to use the initial letter for the name of the court card or ace in their own language, but the English K, Q, J, A are now in addition, internationally used (in Bohemia, for example, cards are either made without any indices at all or with the K, Q, J, A).

Here are some of the indices in use: it should be kept in mind that most cards bearing these indices appeared after 1900; also that except where otherwise stated they appear on French-suited cards.

B, K, θ, A	Greece
H, V, B, 1 or A	Holland
K, D, B, A	Denmark, Germany, Austria and occasionally ex-Empire
K, D, B, Es	Denmark
К, Д, В, Т	Russia

K, D, G, As	Iceland
K, D, J, E	Sweden
K, D, K, 1	Finland
K, D, Kn, 1 or Es or E	Denmark, Norway or Sweden
K, D, W, A	Poland
K, M, B, T	Bulgaria
K, O, U, A	(German suits) Germany
König, Ober, Under	(Swiss suits) Switzerland
K, Q, J, A	Originally English-speaking now universal
K, R, S, 1	Finland
R, D, C, V, A or 1	(French-suit tarots) France or world, Switzerland
R, D, V, A or 1	France, Belgium, Switzerland. Known also in smaller card-producing countries such as Greece and Portugal. Almost as useless a guide as K, Q, J, A!

Spain is perhaps the most helpful to the collector in the matter of dating, for the date of issue appears on many of her packs of cards. For other countries more effort is required and the most valuable aid available on a proportion of European cards is the tax stamp.

Cards have been a source of government revenue for almost as long as they have existed. The tax on them has varied enormously—in England it is one of the few taxes which was gradually reduced from its all time high of 2s. 6d. per pack at the beginning of the nineteenth century until it finally disappeared in the early 1960s.

The usual safeguard taken by tax collectors to prevent evasion was to stamp a card in each pack prior to its being wrapped and offered for sale. This was the system used in England, certainly from about 1711 until 1765 (although the tax had been levied eighty years previously, during the reign of Charles I, there is no exact evidence as to how the law had been enforced before the time of Queen Anne). For those

wishing to study further these early English tax stamps which
were imprinted often indistinctly and not on any specific card
(although the ace of spades ultimately became the 'taxed' card)
a book entitled *British Playing Card Stamp Duties and Their
Authorized Stamps* by John Boynton Kaiser and issued by the
American Philatelic Society is invaluable.

In 1765 a new system of tax collection began. The Stamp
Office printed taxed aces of spades as well as extra duty
wrappers for cardmakers on application. Forgery of such aces
by the cardmakers themselves led to capital punishment: there
is an account of the trial in 1805 of such an unwise person,
Richard Harding, in Gurney Benham's *Playing Cards: The History
and Secrets of the Pack*, and for interest I show in plate VIII
one of the aces thought to have been forged by him. The
earliest type of this style of duty ace helpfully gives the maker's
name but not the figure involved, although the tax was in fact
one shilling. As the tax changed (usually increasing), inscriptions appeared round these aces although the basic design
remained similar until 1828, 'G. III REX' giving way to 'G. IV
REX' in the 1820s. Major recognizable landmarks in this system
appeared as follows:

1776–89: The words SIXPENCE ADDITL. DUTY were added, the
first word on the left reading up and the last two on the right
reading down.

1789–1801: As last but with the words SIX PENCE ADDL.
DUTY also at top of design.

1801–20: Two styles were used in this period. The first
issued was one as last but with ADDL. DUTY SIXPENCE also at
foot of design. After about 1806 this stamp appeared con-
currently with another in which the three 6d. inscriptions have
disappeared and been replaced by ONE SHILLING on the left,
reading up, and AND SIXPENCE on the right, reading down.
DUTY appears at the top.

1820–28: The above two aces seem to have been issued
unchanged for a while in the reign of George IV, but 'GEO IV'
appears on several packs of the period.

1828–62: This duty ace, known as 'Old Frizzle', is a much

more elaborately engraved item than previous aces and was used unchanged through the closing years of George IV, through the reign of William IV and halfway into the reign of Victoria. Apart from its design it bears the distinctive legend DUTY ONE SHILLING at the top.

In 1862 the tax was reduced to threepence but the duty ace was discarded, the tax being paid only on the card wrappers. Each maker was permitted to assert his individuality with regard to the ace of spades which, although no longer taxed, is still decorated.

Cards for export carried no tax so that if the word EXPORTA-TION is found on early aces of spades, the age of the card must be surmised by other means than the above list.

Almost as helpful to collectors were the fiscal authorities of the Austro-Hungarian Empire, particularly during the period between 1800 and the late 1860s when tax stamps included the year of issue.

Mr Fred Taylor, to whom I am most grateful for much of the following matter on Empire tax stamps, tells me that the practice of using tax stamps in Austria began in 1713. The first style (examples of which he cannot trace and I certainly cannot) lasted until 1762. From that date until 1802 the stamps have an irregular shape and indicate their origins by the initial letter of a town (e.g. G for Graz) or state symbol (e.g. the Bohemian lion) plus a number. (See plate VIII.)

After 1802 there was still a variety of shapes and frames in use in the design of the stamps. The content was a letter or letters indicating town or district of origin, plus the amount of tax in kronen plus the word KARTEN and a three- or four-figure date (e.g. 837 or 1837).

For a few years before 1858 a circular stamp in black was also known; this had a filigree decoration which included a reference number but no other inscription. On cards of this period the maker often included his own stamp giving name and date on the ace of hearts as well as the card bearing the tax stamp.

From 1858–77 two black tax stamps which incorporated the two-headed Austrian eagle and also a certain amount of filigree decoration, were used. One merely included a control number in the design, the other bore the inscription K.K. KARTEN-STEMPEL.

The next stamp issued is not of such exact help to the collector, for it was in use for two periods, 1877–81 and 1900–20. It depicts the double-headed Austrian eagle in red enclosed in a blue double border in which the inscription K.K. KARTEN-STEMPEL appears, also in blue. A small central shield bears a control number and the tax appears in outer border at the foot of the stamp. From 1881–1900 the same design was used but the colours were reversed.

In c. 1920 a similar-looking stamp appeared (blue centre, red border) but with a single-headed eagle and re-inscribed ÖSTERR. KARTENSTEMPEL and often having inflated tax values of up to 8000 K.

In 1925 came currency reform and the krone was replaced by groschen and schilling.

In 1932 the double-headed eagle returned (a measure criticized by republicans).

After World War I, the newly independent states each went their own fiscal ways. Czechoslovakia, for instance, replaced the Austrian eagle with a Bohemian lion and the letters R. C. S. on a red background and surrounded this in blue with the traditional double border and the inscription KOLEL Z HRACIC KARET plus the tax value (see plate VIII). Before that war certain parts of the Empire retained independence in the matter but examples of such stamps are extremely rare.

With the coming of the Nazis, the German tax stamp was used in Austria and this state of affairs lasted until 1945 when the single-headed eagle holding hammer and sickle reappeared on Austrian cards and this symbol remained until 1955 when the practice of using such stamps ceased. The Austrian eagle should not be confused with others, particularly with the Prussian one.

From sheer lack of material I cannot trace German tax stamps in use before the nineteenth century. There is, nevertheless, plenty of evidence of various states imposing their own tax

stamps on cards in the nineteenth century prior to the Confederation of North German States in the late 1860s and the
subsequent formation of the German Empire. These are not all
readily identifiable, and often recognition depends upon a
knowledge of either the currency of an area or coat-of-arms
of a specific territory. The Hamburg stamp of the 1850s, for
example, shows the city's badge (a castle with three towers)
over the tax '4.S.' or schilling. In about 1875, when the imperial
currency became that of all Germany, the same castle appears
over '10 p.f.' or pfennig. So far I have not found a stamp in use
during the interim period during which Hamburg joined the
North German Confederation (1868–71) when the currency
used was groschen and thaler as well as kreuzer and gulden,
but I have no doubt that such a stamp exists.

Saxony is another example of a state's coat-of-arms being
employed as sole identity mark. In the early part of the nineteenth century, this badge (under the Saxon crown is a shield
with four horizontal bars crossed by a bend dexter and the
whole is supported by two sheaves) is stamped above the tax
value which was in GR or groschen. By 1850 the currency had
changed to NGR (neugroschen), the sheaves had disappeared
and the words KARTEN STEMPEL introduced. (See plate VIII.)

The Prussian eagle is found in various forms at different
periods and with the appropriate currency for the date. Prior
to the currency reforms carried out on the formation of the
North German Confederation, Prussia's currencies were pfennig and silbergroschen or kreuzer and gulden: the currencies
of the North German Confederation (1866–71) retained kreuzer
and gulden but also used groschen and thaler (Prussian tax
stamps of this period are known inscribed EIN SECHSTEL
THALER—5 GR and EIN DRITTEL THALER—10 GR.). From 1871–
75 the German Empire retained the Confederation's currency,
and from the latter date used pfennig and mark only. The
latest, rather fussily drawn Prussian eagle, with an inscription
KÖENIG R: PREUSSEN, was used as a basis for the next Imperial
German tax stamp, which was inscribed DEUTSCHES REICH plus
the tax value and a control number. This stamp was, until the

end of the First World War, used throughout Germany except in the kingdoms of Bavaria and Württemberg which retained certain independent rights. (See plate VIII.)

In Bavaria, early nineteenth-century tax stamps depicted a simple crown inside two circles of unbroken lines with the name of a Bavarian district (e.g. ISAR KREIS) inscribed round the inside of the border circles, the tax value (4 Ker.) appearing at the foot. Another stamp, apparently of similar period, shows the Bavarian coat-of-arms (a lion within a lozenged shield) under a crown and the letters S. N. which presumably refer to the district 'Schwaben u. Neuburg'. The tax is 8 Ker. (for a tarot pack). Later tax stamps (mid-century—1874) had a slightly more elaborate design, the principal identifying difference being that the inner of the two border circles became a series of dots. The practice of inscribing the name of a district (without reference to the state) was retained (e.g. MITTEL-FRANKEN, U.FRANKEN U. ASCHAFFENBG, SCHWABEN U. NEUBURG, etc.). After 1875, and presumably until World War I, this practice seems to have been reversed and I have only seen tax stamps of this period inscribed BAYERN (with no mention of district) and having their tax in pfennig.

I have described the German tax stamps most commonly used but emphasize that there are numerous others belonging to states both large and small. The safest thing that can be said of them is that if they do not have the DEUTSCHES REICH inscription, they belong to the age before Prussia organized the unification of Germany.

After World War I a much more simply drawn angular eagle, without an imperial crown but with DEUTSCHES REICH in gothic lettering, was used until the swastika of the Nazis was incorporated in the late 1930s. Since World War II no tax stamps have been used in Western Germany, nor, so far as I know, in the Eastern sector.

Most of Italy has, since 1862, used the same tax stamp throughout its regions: certainly uniformity can be observed as soon as a territory finally became united to Italy proper. Before the unification the different states used their individual systems and I have not been able to discover sufficient material to warrant any categorical statements. Currency and an historical encyclopaedia with which to explore the intrigues and vicissitudes of the pre-united Italian government are the only aids I can suggest. Some of the currencies found on these old stamps are as follows:

bajocchi	Romagna and Papal States
soldi	Tuscany
grana	Naples and Sicily

Otherwise centesimi and lire were used.

Tax stamps on cards must have been one of the first pre-occupations of a united Italy, for the first general stamp authorized bears the inscription REGNO D'ITALIA LEGGE 21 SETT 1862, plus the tax at the base: the whole inscription surrounds a seated allegorical figure. The tax was 50 centesimi for tarots and 30 centesimi for other cards. This tax stamp seems to have lasted about twenty years when it was supplanted by a head with a winged helmet. This was depicted in one of a number of colours on a white background and surrounded by a plain circle: the inscription reads REGNO D'ITALIA plus the sum of the tax (as above). Sometimes, on the same card, a stamp like a postmark is added giving date (usually the last two figures of the year and very indistinct) and city of origin. The actual stamp cannot have been used for long for the head soon achieved a lined background (the duty remaining the same) which was also known with the extra 'postmark' of the '80s and '90s. Between the World Wars, the head with lined background was retained, but the duty rose to three lire. In the 1920s all necessity for speculation was ended by the date of issue being plainly printed on the card having a tax stamp: this form of REGNO D'ITALIA stamp was used right up to the end of the war. After a short interim a similar stamp was employed inscribed REPUBBLICA ITALIANA plus tax which started at LIRE CENTO, but in 1955 was raised to LIRE TRECENTO which must make Italian cards among the most heavily taxed in the world.

The pre-Revolution tax stamp on Russian cards has been mentioned, with the badge of the Foundling Hospital on the ace of diamonds (all proceeds of the tax went to the upkeep of the hospital) but even though the pelican caring for its young is a distinctive device, its design can rarely tell you more than that the cards belonged to Imperial Russia. Other countries too have their own devices and designs but it would involve a great deal of patient and detailed research to produce anything like a useful list.

A final guide to the identification of playing cards which would be invaluable to any collector, would be a complete list of cardmakers and their dates. This work would fill a book by itself and would probably never be complete. Notwithstanding, it is well worth while to keep a record of every maker's name that you come across with any scraps of information you have been able to glean about him. Today the cardmakers of the world are depressingly few and display monopolistic tendencies although they produce many beautiful cards. B. P. Grimaud of Paris is perhaps the oldest, having roots in the eighteenth century, but Ferd. Piatnik of Vienna has a history going back to 1824, while De La Rue of London had its beginnings only eight years later. A.S.S. of Germany is the descendant of a multitude of nineteenth-century firms from all over the country and represents countless takeovers, mergers and reorganizations. Some of the nineteenth-century giants have, however, fallen by the wayside, finding the ways of mass production too overwhelming in competition. The Uffenheimers of Vienna, A. B. Göbl of Munich, Dondorf and Wüst of Frankfurt, Wokaun of Prague, the Royal Manufactory of Madrid, and Daveluy of Bruges, have all disappeared, leaving the playing card scene all the poorer. One that has survived is the Spanish Fournier of Vitoria who continues to produce beautiful cards for export all over the world.

In the bibliography that follows I have referred where relevant to sources which provide dates for at least a limited number of makers. The trouble is tracing the books themselves.

I make no apology for including one or two items which are rarely found outside museums or their libraries; a serious student can always seek them out. The first work mentioned is in this category and contains an unparalleled amount of erudite and informed commentary on the cards described.

Playing Cards of Various Ages and Countries: Selected from the Collection of Lady Charlotte Schreiber: John Murray, London. In three volumes: Vol. I. English, Scottish, Dutch and Flemish (1892). Vol. II. French and German (1893). Vol. III. Swiss, Swedish, Russian, Polish, Italian, Spanish and Portuguese, together with a supplement of other countries (1895).

The cards illustrated in this enormous work can be seen in the Print Room of the British Museum but for full appreciation of their qualities and history the book itself provides invaluable information.

Catalogue of the Collection of Playing Cards bequeathed to the Trustees of the British Museum by the late Lady Charlotte Schreiber: Compiled by Freeman M. O'Donoghue, F.S.A.: Longmans, Green and Co. and others, London; 1901.

Although without illustrations, this book is essential for reference. It describes with short comments the many hundreds of packs (all pre-1900) in the collection. It is a wonderful aid towards dating and placing many old packs and is very good on makers.

Catalogue of the Collection of Playing Cards of Various Ages and Countries: formed by Henry D. Phillips (Master of the Worshipful Company of Makers of Playing Cards 1896–7). Printed for private circulation; 1903.

This collection, while not so extensive as that at the British Museum, is in many ways complementary to it. It is housed in the Guildhall, London. The book is much rarer than the catalogue of the Schreiber collection but if obtained is most useful; it is good on makers.

A History of Playing and Other Cards in the British Museum, accompanied by a Concise General History of the Subject: by William Hughes Willshire, M.D.: Edinburgh; 1876.

This describes the cards in the British Museum prior to the acquisition of the Schreiber collection. A most useful work but unfortunately difficult to obtain. It is good on makers.

A History of Playing Cards and a Bibliography of Cards and Gaming: by Catherine Perry Hargrave. Compiled and illustrated from the old cards and books in the collection of the United States Playing Card Company in Cincinnati: Houghton Mifflin; Boston and New York; 1930. 456 pages.

It is odd that all the best books on playing cards are about specific collections. This is a beautifully and lavishly illustrated work which is scarce and expensive but which is particularly good on American cards; it has a 78-page bibliography and cards from hundreds of packs are illustrated. It is not infallible but what is? It is good on makers.

The History of Playing Cards, with Anecdotes of their Use in Conjuring, Fortune-telling and Card-sharping: edited by E. S. Taylor and others: John Camden Hotten, London; 1865. 529 pages.

This contains many interesting quotations and illustrations; some conclusions are questionable but it is worth having.

Facts and Speculations on the Origins and History of Playing Cards: by William Andrew Chatto: John Russell Smith, London; 1848. 343 pages.

Very good on Indian and Persian cards and puts forward an ingenious case for the oriental origins of cards. It is illustrated and is good on etymology all through.

Old and Curious Playing Cards, Their History and Types from Many Countries and Periods: by H. T. Morley, B.SC.(ARCH.), F.R.HIST.S., F.S.P.: B. T. Batsford Ltd, London; 1931. 235 pages.

The chief value of this work lies in the illustrations of many cards not recorded elsewhere so far as I know. The cards illustrated were mainly from the author's own collection.

Playing Cards: Their History and Secrets: by W. Gurney Benham: Ward Lock, London, 1931. Reprinted by Spring Books, London, n.d. but probably during the 1950s.

This is a most uneven book on cards, leaving out vast territories of the subject but it does contain a great deal of useful information about certain French and English cards and their makers and is fully illustrated.

War Cards: A Prolusion: by Melbert B. Cary, Jr: Press of the Woolly Whale, New York; 1937.

A fully illustrated and beautifully produced work on a single theme as illustrated on playing cards.

The Devil's Picture Books: A History of Playing Cards by Mrs John King Van Rensselaer: T. Fisher Unwin, London; 1892.

A rather uneven but not uninteresting general history, nicely illustrated.

Prophetical Educational and Playing Cards: by Mrs John King Van Rensselaer: Hurst and Blackett, London; 1912.

Of most use to those interested in the possibility of tracing the history of tarot cards back to the temples of ancient Egypt but it does contain matter of more contemporary interest.

Absolute Key to Occult Science; The Tarot of the Bohemians; The Most Ancient Book in the World. For the exclusive use of initiates: by 'Papus': Chapman and Hall, London; 1892.

Perhaps the best known of countless books on the same subject; taking or leaving it is a matter of personal taste.

Explanatory Notes of a Pack of Cavalier Playing Cards, Temp. Charles II, forming a Complete Political Satire of the Commonwealth: by Edmund Goldsmid, F.R.H.S., F.S.A.(SCOT.): E. & G. Goldsmid; Edinburgh; 1886.

See previous reference on page 151.

Graphis 33: Graphis Press, Zurich; 1950.

Pages 386–95 of this issue of the magazine are devoted to an excellent article on Indian playing cards, with illustrations, by R. von Leyden.

Charta Lusoria: by Eberhard Pinder: Basoderm, G.M.B.H., Biberach an der Riss; 1961.

This deals with a few representative cards from all areas and ages in an authoritative manner. A 'must' on Indian cards even if the German has to be translated word by word. Good colour illustrations.

Les Cartes à Jouer du XIVe au XXe Siècle: by Henry-René d'Allemagne: Hachette, Paris; 1906.

This mammoth work in two volumes, consisting of more than 1,000 pages and even more illustrations, must for many years remain a standard work on French cards: a wonderful but very rare work which provides an enormous amount of information and is incomparable on French makers.

Origine des Cartes à Jouer: Recherches nouvelles sur les naibis, les tarots et sur les autres espèces de cartes: by R. Merlin: Paris; 1869.

A first-class and scholarly approach to the subject, with a mass of good illustration; in particular, this work assesses all the quoted early sources of references to playing cards from the thirteenth century onwards and finds that most of them are in fact quotations or hearsay.

Recherches sur les Cartiers et les Cartes à Jouer à Grenoble: by Edmond Maigniep: Imprimerie Joseph Allier, Grenoble, 1887.

A small book but lavishly illustrated and full of detailed

information; this is a typical example of many nineteenth-century booklets dealing with cards and cardmakers of various parts of France.

Les Cartes à Jouer et la Cartomancie: by P. Boiteau d'Ambly: Hachette, Paris; 1854.

Similar in character to the edition in English edited by the Rev. Taylor and containing many identical illustrations: it includes an account of Etteilla's method of fortune-telling, i.e. the principal eighteenth-century tarot fashion of cartomancy.

Katalog der im Germanischen Museum befindlichen Kart:nspiele und Spielkarten: Nuremberg; 1886.

A nice item for reference to many early German cards and makers.

Deutsche Spielkarten: by Otto Reisig: Bibliographisches Institut, Leipzig; 1935.

An excellent little book dealing with German cards in general terms by a real authority.

Münchner Spielkarten um 1500: by Hellmut Rosenfeld: Bielefeld; 1958.

A profusely illustrated account of early German playing cards, with twenty-four pages of text.

Speelkarten: by Han Janssen: C.A.J. van Dishoeck, Bussum; 1965.

Even if the Dutch language is unfamiliar, this little book contains illustrations of hundreds of cards not to be found elsewhere.

Of Carving, Cards and Cookery: Virginia and Harold Wayland: Raccoon Press, Arcadia, California; 1962.

A delightful book built round the Carving cards of Lenthall's list (see page 139) and containing reproductions of all fifty-two cards.

Researches into the History of Playing Cards, with illustrations of the origin of printing and engraving on wood: by Samuel Weller Singer: London; 1816.

An early but serious illustrated study of the subject.

Many other books of varying length and quality exist on the subject of playing cards; I have merely mentioned those most likely to provide helpful information to a serious collector. In a slightly different category are the editions of cards in book form; the Cavalier playing cards would fall into this class only if the pack were reproduced exactly. Many antique non-standard cards were issued in book form, usually with a commentary, and are easily recognizable as such. There are also innumerable books and articles on games and fortune-telling, offering pet theories on all aspects of cards: I have not dealt very fully with the subject of fortune-telling cards because there is plenty of reference material available to a collector of such cards. I leave it to the judgement of individual collectors as to which they find most useful but in this subject personal preference must play a large part; much of the charm and pleasure in collecting playing cards must always lie in the individuality of choice which it permits.